Divorce, Empowerment, and Attorneys: What You Need to Know

By Nadine Larsson

© 2010 first edition as You Can Do This!
Divorce, Empowerment, and Attorneys
a primer by Nadine Larsson (zine)

© 2011 second edition as You Can Do This!
Divorce, Empowerment, and Attorneys,
a primer by Nadine Larsson
ISBN 978-0-9836310-0-2

© 2012 third edition as Divorce, Empowerment, and Attorneys
What You Need to Know
by Nadine Larsson (E-book)
ISBN 978-0-9836310-1-9

©2012 third edition as Divorce, Empowerment, and Attorneys:
What You Need to Know
by Nadine Larsson
ISBN 978-0-9836310-2-6
The author reserves all rights. No part of this book may be used or
reproduced in any manner without written permission, except in the
case of brief quotations embodied in reviews.

If you would like to contact the author,
you can write her at Nadine.larsson@gmail.com.

Editing and design by Composed Editing.
Kylin Larsson, editor, may be contacted at
kylin@composedediting.com.

You never change things by fighting the existing reality.
To change something,
build a new model
that makes the old one
obsolete.

R. Buckminster Fuller

Dedication

This book is dedicated to my son, Lars, and my daughter, Alexis, who scooped me up and carried me with them emotionally until I was ready to stand on my own two feet again. Thank you, my darlings.

And, to my daughter-in-law, Kylin, my second daughter, for maintaining her professionalism during the process of developing and copy editing my manuscript, and for all of those little ways in which she continues to nurture and support me and the rest of our family.

Acknowledgements

While staying at Paradise Lodge on Mount Rainier, I chanced upon a woman by the name of Mimi Welch. She and her mother were walking on the path in front of me. Her mother had just been given some health news of an unpleasant nature. When I sent Mimi the photos I'd taken, I received a thank you note in which she added, "We are lucky to hear your voice." Every time I've considered giving up on this piece, because I've evolved away from the pain of this experience, I've remembered Mimi's words.

I grew up in Potlatch, Washington, and Linda Jarvis, along with her sisters Wendy and Barbara, lived on the road just behind our house. Our backyards ran into one another. Linda and her sisters added to what was for me an idyllic childhood: we reenacted game shows like *Queen for a Day* and *Jeopardy*; we created paper houses and imaginative scenarios for our ceramic figurines; and pilfered wild strawberries from Mrs.Carlson's apple orchard. Linda was my friend all through school and when I most needed a friend, and a safe harbor, she provided both. Thank you, Linda, for still being my friend, even after living with me for more than a month.

Contents

Forward 1

Part I: Why I Left My Marriage 3

Part II: Preparing for Divorce 11

    How to Stay Safe 18

    How to Stay Safe When Leaving an Abusive Relationship 19

    If You are Attacked 20

Part III: Snapshot of Misalignment 21

Part IV: Tools of Realignment 25

.... 25

Personal Space and Feng Shui 31

    Family and Past 36

    Wealth 36

    Health 37

    Helpful People 38

    Children and Creativity 38

    Knowledge and Spirituality 39

    Fame and Success 40

    Career and Life Path 41

    Relationships and Intimacy 41

Physical self-care 45

Energy Work 53

Visual Journaling 57

SoulCollage® 61

Intuitive Counseling 67

Meditation 71

Healing through Archetypes and Chakras 73

Affirmations 81

Tarot 85

Mythic Journaling 89

Astrology 93

My Favorite Tarot Reader 99

Body Work, Again: Colon Hydrotherapy 101

EFT 105

Dance 111

Epilogue 115

Learning…and, living! 117

Helpful Resources 119

Books Referenced 121

Tarot Decks Referenced..124

Forward

This is the third edition of the book I originally named You Can Do This! *Divorce, Empowerment and Attorneys--What You Need to Know—a primer by Nadine Larsson.* I wanted to call this edition How Not to get Screwed Over in Your Divorce, because that's basically what Parts I and II are about, but that sounded too much like it may have a lot of dry humor and even now I can't quite muster much humor around the part of my life told in Parts I and II. Part III carries a couple of memories I find to be somewhat telling, I think, of this part of my life—remnants, so to speak. Part IV begins my recovery from a tumultuous marriage and violating divorce. Although I found many of the tools mentioned here while my divorce was still in process, it's taken me a long time to trust myself again, to value myself, and to listen to myself enough to get the most out of these tools. My hope is that you find something in these pages to use as anchor or catalyst, whichever you need while going through a difficult time. You may want to try some of the recovery tools I enjoyed exploring.

Please note that if you have been the victim of violence, Part 1 may describe a violent incident in terms too graphic for you and may bring up uncomfortable memories for you. It may be that you will want to ask a close friend to preview that chapter on your behalf. Or, you may want to skip that part all together. No matter your choice, please know that, by virtue of the fact you have chosen to read this book at all, you are protected, safe and loved and I reach out to you now to put my virtual arms around you in a big hug.

I read the books. I tried to educate and prepare myself for the process. He had the law degree. He had the books. He was an attorney who specialized in family law. He sounded like he would protect my interests. He sounded like he would provide me with good representation. I was mistaken. Especially where there has been any incident of domestic abuse, here is what you need to know.

Part I:
Why I Left My Marriage

*O*n Tuesday, October the fifth, 2004, the man I loved, who I had married not once, but twice over the period of twenty-five years, forced my mouth open and scraped a fork along the pink tissue of my throat like a dog digging for a bone and made it a chopped-up mess.

He had always been a violent and angry man, but it never occurred to me with any sense of real possibility that he could become violent toward me. He broke my daughter's cherished dollhouse that I'd spent weeks of my evenings making for her. He kicked the doors in our home. He once squealed the tires in the IKEA parking lot, alarming everyone and bringing security over, just because someone had taken his parking space. Because he couldn't find a parking space so that we could visit the museum, he drove erratically through the streets of a little town in Sweden called Örebro. I'm serious. Everyone jumped out of the way; it was like being in some kind of action movie.

Once, while we were on vacation in Sweden and driving with my stepson and his wife, somebody cut off my husband on the roadway and he was bound and determined to catch up with them. As he sped forward, my daughter-in-law became white as a sheet. I shoved a newspaper over my head in an attempt to divert her attention from what was for her, and for all of us, a scary situation over which we had absolutely no control.

The incident with the fork down my throat was not the first time my husband had been physically abusive. We owned a merchant vessel when we were first married, an old freighter called the TUKWILA CHIEF. I was onboard for some nine months while my son was in kindergarten. We were in Bogotá and we had invited the local shipping agent and his wife to dinner. There had been several courses served to us in the main salon, served with the alcohol accompaniment appropriate to each course. I don't remember the reason for our argument. I only recall him kicking me. I remember cowering in the salon with my knees in front of my face to prevent him from hitting or kicking me again. I think it was only once and it left no exterior bruises, and then he left me alone. I was devastated. I called my mother the next day, and I nearly flew back home. I had never in my life been physically threatened in any way. My husband didn't recall kicking me and was contrite. I told him then, if he ever hit me again I would be gone. Then, I completely, and conveniently, forgot that scene for years.

I recently read a saying about how things happen. If something happens once, you know it will never happen again. If something happens twice, you can guarantee it will happen a third time.

I remember very little of the night of the incident in Lynnwood, Washington, in 2004. I'm told this is how the body and mind cope with trauma. The only thing I remember, although I didn't at first, is that my husband held me with one hand behind my back while he reached behind me into the drawer of the china cabinet, forced my mouth open, and shoved something inside it. He grated it against the inside of my throat while he shouted, "I've been spoon feeding you information for years." I remember being irritated at the grating sound because it was so loud I couldn't hear the rest of what my husband was saying and I wanted to hear the words, all the words.

When he let me up, I saw the china cabinet in front of me, with its Royal Copenhagen cups and saucers in the lovely seagull pattern that I'd bought for my mother. I don't know what happened between the time I saw the china cabinet, still holding my treasured possessions, and then looking again to see its contents demolished on the floor, but I think that my husband probably kicked me because I was bruised all over. I remember feeling very dazed, standing and looking at him, and that's when he punched me in the face. I ran from my home.

My stepson was staying with us at the time, while he was completing a postgraduate law class at the University of Washington. I drove to a nearby parking area and waited until my stepson returned from classes. Then I went back into the house and I packed some of my belongings. I was certainly in shock because I only packed a skirt, a pair of jeans, and tennis shoes. No underwear. No business clothing to wear to the office.

When I returned to the house, my stepson was at the stove making soup. I had to walk past my husband to get something out of the laundry room. Instead of cowering, this time I looked directly at him and I told him I never, ever, wanted to see his face or hear the sound of his voice again.

As a matter of curiosity, I opened the drawer of the china cabinet, the drawer it sounded like my husband had reached into for his weapon, hoping that I would find the weapon itself. Eerily, the knife of the carving set was in the drawer. Not the set. Not the fork. Not the black case where it normally sat along with the knife sharpener and the carving fork, but all alone. Waiting?

I hadn't realized that I was bleeding. I drove myself to the Albertson's parking lot a few blocks from my house and I just sat there, trying to get my bearings, trying to figure out what to do next. My daughter, who was living in Olympia at the time, called me on my cell phone. She had just called home to touch base and to say hello and, when her dad answered, he told her that I wasn't home and that we had had a fight. My daughter, who had noted her father's previous acts of verbal abuse and violence toward objects, asked, "Did you hit her?" He'd said, "No," and then she phoned me. Although I said I was fine, she didn't believe me. I did tell her that her dad had hit me. "Just stay there in the parking lot," she said, "I'm coming up."

I waited. I think I slept. I took a photograph of myself (I'd seen this done by several people to document fun things and I had my camera with me. What better way to document this incident?) I don't know why I took the photo, but I'm glad I did. It could have come in handy had we gone to court, which we didn't. This comment, by itself, is the one reason I chose to write out these memories.

My daughter arrived at the parking lot. We switched places. She drove my car. Neither one of us realized how badly I was bleeding. Thank God she demanded to take me to the emergency room to make sure I was as "fine" as I said I was.

We drove to St. Peter's Hospital in Olympia. On the way, I told my daughter how badly my throat hurt, as though I had strep throat. I used to get strep throat once a year, but not since I started wearing a hat during the cold months. I anticipated the doctor could give me something for my strep throat, and then I could go to my daughter's to sleep. I didn't know if my husband would try to find me or not, but I thought I would at least be safe in Olympia that night.

I was right. Aside from a couple of messages, my husband didn't seem to be concerned about me. He left me one voicemail in a very soothing voice, as though he were talking to a child: "I hope you come home soon, honey. I turned the heat up and the house is all warm for you." It was so very eerie that it scared me and I erased it. I wish I had kept the messages and the cell phone to use as evidence in court. Perhaps then the legal outcome would have been to my benefit, instead of my ex-husband's.

I didn't remember anything about the incident until I was at the hospital. Once the doctor looked at my throat he told me we would have to report this to the police. He wanted me to give them my statement. I told him I was not prepared to do that. The only way he would respect my privacy and keep the police out of it was if I promised to go to my regular physician within the next three days. He told me that whatever had happened to my throat was no infection. He had no way of knowing how it happened, but my throat was all chewed up and it was badly infected. I would have died of blood poisoning before morning.

It was about half an hour or so after the doctor told me what my throat looked like that I remembered. I remembered my husband shouting at me, and I remembered how difficult it had been to hear his words. Over the next few days, I remembered most of the incident that night.

The bleeding turned out to be from an incision that was just half an inch from my spinal cord. There was so much glass on the floor at the house that I probably either fell or was kicked and rammed up against a shard of glass. The cut was mended with just a few stitches. I bled all over both seats of my car, though, and it took the Mercedes dealership in Tacoma about an hour to remove the bloodstains.

Although I loved my husband very much, I knew that I could never really trust him again. I knew, too, that if I lived without trust I would eat myself alive. I would make myself physically ill. It also occurred to me that perhaps the next time we argued, I would physically defend myself and I might kill him. What if I landed in prison? Just this thought alone demanded that I end the relationship at any cost.

I did stay with my daughter that night, and I was raised out of a sound sleep by a call on my cell phone and my husband screaming, "I can't find my wallet. I need my (expletive) wallet. You SOB, you took my (expletive) wallet. Don't you ever come back here." We lived in the house that my mother had signed over to us with only a little of our own investment. In essence, he was telling me not to come back to the home that he had because of me. Later in the day, this time in a normal tone of voice, he left the message, "I don't know how I could have done that to you. I love you so much." I also deleted that message.

I went to see my regular physician as I promised the emergency room doctor I would. She told me that either I had to go to the police or she would. The infection in my throat was still raging and she gave me the strongest antibiotic she could. As for me, I walked into the Lynnwood police department and filed my report. They asked for photographs. My husband was arrested about thirty minutes later, at his job, for second-degree felony assault.

I was fortunate enough to have an old school chum who lived in Tacoma and who had an extra room available until I found an apartment. When I first went to her house, I couldn't stay by myself. I was nervous if she went outside. I wanted the curtains closed. I couldn't take a shower, because I was too scared to be alone. I couldn't fathom this kind of violation of my person, especially by someone whom I loved. I reasoned that person must hate me; I must have no worth whatsoever; to that person, I must be worthless.

Since I didn't want my husband to know where I was, and all of our credit card and bank accounts were online, I remember charging things in Seattle or in Olympia, anywhere except for Tacoma. I didn't go to my office for several days because I wasn't able to sit still or concentrate. I couldn't stop shaking. On the day that I tried to return to work, my birthday, my husband sent me flowers: lilies. The selection was beautiful, especially in its irony. I panicked. Was he outside? Had he watched me come to work? Would he kill me on my way back to the car? There was no card. There was never any "I'm sorry," not that it would likely have made any difference. I was absolutely terrified and acted hysterically. Fortunately, I had vacation time and my boss let me take two weeks off.

One of my co-workers walked me to my car and I told him the short story before heading home, knowing that word would go around the office, and I'd not need to say anything else. The initial reaction of my coworker to my story, and to my irrational behavior, was that I was likely overreacting to the situation. After all, there were no visible signs of any abuse except my swollen nose--not that hitting someone in the face wasn't bad-- but things can happen during times of stress. I rolled up my sleeves and exposed my bruises. I explained how the tissue on the inside of my throat came to look like hamburger. I asked if he wanted to see that, too. My coworker recoiled

At my doctor's insistence, I made an appointment with the psychologist that she worked with on a referral basis. I only saw her two or three times. She diagnosed me with post-traumatic stress disorder. My whole way of life, the way that I had planned my life, was gone. In its place: loneliness. Betrayal. The stupidity of love had dulled my common sense. My own foolishness for having worn rose-colored glasses so often that I hadn't considered this as a real possibility. My foolishness was gone. I couldn't recall everything that happened that night, but my body could. Slowly, as is apparently the case with PTSD, many things from that night have come filtering back for me to look at. Not all, but some.

     My friend went to work on Monday morning, leaving me alone at the house. I watched television to keep myself company. I saw a black Mercedes pull up in front of the house. My husband drove a black Mercedes. Too scared to cry and shaking uncontrollably, I called the police. "My husband is trying to kill me," I sobbed, as I crouched in the corner of the guest room. I moved anything that could reveal my presence away from any window in case he looked inside. The Mercedes pulled away just as three police cars drove up out front of my friend's house. I couldn't stop crying. The officer in charge took one look at me, still badly bruised and my nose puffed up like a prizefighter's. "It's okay." he told me. "Call us whenever you need to." My friend's neighbor across the street, a retired police officer, was able to shed light on the incident by telling the police that the car was driven by a young man who stopped the car, got something out of the trunk, and then pulled away.

Part II:
Preparing for Divorce

I found the attorney to represent me through a referral from a friend. This friend is very kind and I recalled that her brother was an attorney; however, as he told me, I was not in his jurisdiction and I was referred to an attorney who was. I wish I had taken the time to speak with a few attorneys in the area and to have asked the Prosecuting Attorney's office for a referral as well. My divorce was handled in a manner that leads me to believe that women are better attorneys than men when it comes to matters of the heart. The attorney for my husband represented her client very well.

I originally wanted to file for a legal separation so I could have time to calm down, to get my bearings and consider my options. This was a few days after the incident and my nose was still swollen. The attorney told me he could be of no help unless I wanted a divorce. "What if he had killed you? Do you realize how close he came to killing you? Would you seriously consider going back to him?"

My attorney said a divorce and the possible trial to accompany it would be the only course of action with which he could assist me. I paid the retainer with my husband's credit card. I suppose that, in a way, he was really working for my husband. That's pretty much how the actual decree seemed to work out too.

I remember very little about the visits to my attorney. On the advice of my attorney, I got a restraining order against my husband. I didn't want anything to do with him because I felt that, if I heard the sound of his voice, I would have given in and gone back to him. I knew I couldn't allow myself to do that. This may seem odd to the reader, but this was familiar territory to me. My husband was a man with whom I'd shared good times and bad for a quarter of a century, and I loved him very much.

I wish I would have asked my attorney to explain to me exactly what I could expect to occur during the settlement conference. My attorney asked me to give him a list of things I wanted. Back at work and now with a backlog, I'd been busy and I hadn't had a chance to put anything together until finally, the day before the conference, I faxed my attorney a wish list. I thought my list would be provided to the judge in some formal way. The list included my husband readying our home for sale, selling it, paying our mutual debts (which I listed) along with a couple of other items, like giving me some family photos and home videos. The last sentence of this little epistle stated how I felt on that particular day: "In many ways, I feel like I've been let out of a prison." Although this was what I was feeling that day, it was a statement that was not worthy of the relationship nor the years that I shared with my husband and I honestly think a female attorney would have had better sense than to leave that in when we went to court. I was extremely embarrassed and disappointed to see it clearly listed and presented, unedited, to the judge and to my husband and his attorney. I felt that it was a clear violation of my emotional space. That sentence was part of my grieving for a life of which I no longer had an option.

Nothing prepared me for the experience of the settlement conference itself. My lawyer didn't prepare me for it, and he certainly didn't protect me. For the settlement conference, my attorney and I went in an anteroom of the court while my husband and his attorney remained in the courtroom. The judge went over my list with my husband first, then came to the anteroom. The first words that he said were, "Your husband doesn't agree with this list and wants to take this to court." My immediate response was, "Okay, fine." My attorney then produced the photograph that I'd taken of myself on the night of the abuse incident. Negotiations began.

My attorney simply watched, allowing me to sign away my major asset, my house, with absolutely no strings attached. No lien, no promissory note, no fail-safes or assurances of any kind. He did say, "I don't know. I don't trust this guy." Wow! That is a major understatement. As for me, I just wanted out of that relationship and I didn't want my husband coming after me. Or, if he did, I wanted to be able to stand in my own power and not have any guilt because I'd taken something that didn't belong to me, or of which I was not worthy. I had chosen this person, and stayed with him, for a reason. Part of that reason was that my self-esteem was in the toilet. And, I was working so much that I just didn't stop to really look at my life. I honestly think a female attorney would have realized my vulnerability and used this argument to guide me toward a more realistic settlement.

I had asked my attorney during the selection process if he had handled domestic violence cases. As I recall, he said domestic violence cases comprised most of his caseload. At the end of the settlement conference, the actual settlement is read out in court along with relevant questions, such as do you want to change to your maiden name, and whether anything has been omitted. At this point, I considered the air miles on our British Airways card, and I decided that I would rather have my soon to be ex-husband flying around the world instead of lurking anywhere near my world.

When my husband sold the house and failed to pay the debts, the creditors came after me. I was then informed that the decree in the Superior Court was not binding on any of the credit card companies since they are covered by the Federal Court system. One by one, the creditors began garnisheeing my wages, until I was finally forced to file for bankruptcy.

Reflecting on my experience, these are some things you need to know in order not to get screwed in your divorce:

1. Keep all photographs, cell phone records, and answering machine records.

2. Gather support. Get into therapy if you can afford it. Admit that you need an objective ear. Join with other women doing something. It doesn't matter so much what it is. The most important thing is that they love and nurture you and they are glad you are in their company. If your experience is anything less, join a different group. Stop. Listen to yourself. Bother to

hear your inner voice. Learn to trust yourself. For some, it's a premier performance. For others, it's a refresher course. It doesn't matter. Just learn to trust yourself.

3. Go slowly. For me, it was like I had some kind of disease that I needed to rid myself of so that I could move on with my life. Hindsight is (of course) always clearer, but I think I would have fared better had I taken the time to consider my options. But, I must say, I think it's typical of a battering situation when you're so afraid of reconciliation and yet so longing for it. In my haste, I used an ax, destroying my entire way of life, when what I really needed then was a scalpel to remove the toxic portion of my life, my spouse, and some peripheral tissue.

4. Shop for your attorney. Have free consultations of at least two, and better yet, three attorneys to gauge the best fit for you and your circumstance. My new neighbor, a criminal attorney named Natalie, adds: "Your attorney should be considering what your goals are and advising you as to all of your options, including a legal separation instead of dissolution if that's what you want. A legal separation can later be converted to a dissolution proceeding by motion and this often gives you and your attorney an opportunity to become fully versed on your personal financial situation and future needs. Trust yourself. If it doesn't feel like a good fit, then it probably isn't and you should keep looking."

5. Tell your attorney you are at your most vulnerable and you need an attorney who will protect you, including protecting you from yourself.

6. Ask your attorney what to expect at the next step and take notes. Try to visualize this next step, the outcome you want, and picture living with the outcome.

In addition to the above, here are some words of wisdom from a friend of mine, Trish Holmes of Sound Financial Concepts:

1. Get credit reports from all three major agencies for you and your spouse.

2. List every open credit account and whether it is joint or individual.

3. Close joint accounts and reopen in just your name with an entirely different number. If there are balances, either take responsibility for that entire balance and move it to a separate number or make sure it is closed to further credit. If you do not close those joint accounts—even if they are awarded to the spouse—you could be held responsible for any future debts they charge. If you can, pay off any balance remaining on any credit account. If you get a settlement from equity in your home, use it to pay off the credit that was used. Remember there are eleven states that are community property states. Once you get married, you can be held accountable for the debts of your spouse whether you signed the credit application or not.

4. Revoke in writing any authorization for your spouse to use any of your accounts. Keep copies of these letters for at least seven years.

5. Close bank accounts. They will not let you remove a spouse's name, but they can't stop you from closing the account. If the spouse is awarded the debts, be aware that you could still end up responsible if they declare bankruptcy or die.

6. Make sure you have life insurance on the spouse you are divorcing and that you call your agent to have the ownership of that policy in your name. Have this granted in the divorce

decree that you are the owner and they have to pay the premium or at least half.

7. Contact all credit companies and financial accounts to advise them of your divorce.

8. If you had a prenuptial agreement, be aware that acquired debts will become community debts unless it is clearly spelled out in that prenuptial agreement. For example, any IRS debt has to be paid; IRS debts, in most cases, cannot be included in bankruptcy.

The YWCA website has some valuable tips about how to stay safe, which I include on the following pages.

How to Stay Safe

1. Keep a cell phone available to call 911. Many local YWCAs offer a free cell phone for this purpose.

2. If you are in a violent relationship and are afraid, ask neighbors or nearby friends to call the police if they hear violence – you may not be able to call. You may also want to teach your children to phone 911 or get help if it will not seriously endanger them.

3. Be aware of your surroundings. Stay in rooms with more than one exit so you do not get trapped in a room. Stay out of rooms with any sharp objects.

4. Use your judgment and intuition.

5. Keep an emergency bag with supplies in case you have to leave quickly.

6. Learn the signs of violence & get out when you see tension building.

7. Remove all sharp objects from countertops and line of sight.
8. Let trusted friends, family and work know what is happening so they can be there for you.

9. Make copies of important records like bank accounts and financial information, birth certificates, Social Security cards, insurance agent, etc. Give them to someone you trust or hide them, preferably outside your home.

How to Stay Safe When Leaving an Abusive Relationship

1. Only let trusted friends & family know your plan.

2. If you are employed, talk to security at your job or your boss about the situation, so they can help you develop a work safety plan.

3. Gather and make copies of important documents. Your local YWCA may be able to provide you an essential document list to help you plan what you will need.

4. Take your children and pets.

5. Rehearse your departure.

6. Plan your escape route.

7. Notify your children's school if the other parent is not supposed to pick up children, and not to release information about your address or phone number. Some states allow you to use a state post office box number to protect your address.

8. Vary your routes and times to and from work.

9. Consider changing your work location.

10. Remember that no one deserves to be abused!

If You are Attacked

1. If an attack is in progress or about to happen, call 911. Protect yourself, children and pets.

2. Police policy is to arrest someone if they find that an assault has occurred.

3. If they arrest an abuser, the police should call a domestic violence advocate. Many local YWCAs have advocates, but if yours doesn't the police will know whom to contact.

4. Go to a hospital emergency room if injuries are severe. Ask them to document injuries. Ask a nurse to call an advocate to provide support and help you with immediate safety planning.

5. Consider a domestic violence protection order.

6. Create a safety plan.

7. Document injuries with photos and witnesses. You may need them later.

National Domestic Violence Hotline: 1-800-799-SAFE (7233); TTY 1-800-787-3224

Contact your local YWCA for more information.

Part III:
Snapshot of Misalignment

*A*s a victim of emotional abuse, I hadn't realized how the feelings of powerlessness and inequity can be so insidious that we don't know we're suffering from them. We open up so much when we're in love, and it's so easy to compromise to the point where we negotiate ourselves away from our true selves.

As an aside, I recall an incident that happened when I related a story to my husband. My husband and I visited my in-laws in Sweden nearly every year. At the end of our stay, my mother-in-law, in her eighties and nineties, would ask me to clean their apartment. My sister-in-law, who lived nearby, came in once a week to clean and it was my pleasure to give her a break from this little task. When I cleaned, I cleaned everything from floor to ceiling. During one of the last times I was fortunate enough to visit my in-laws, my father-in-law commented that his daughter was not as thorough, that she didn't vacuum the baseboards or the tops of doors.

I took this as a compliment. I later shared this compliment with my husband. When I told him, though, my husband interpreted his father's statement to be a condescending comment from a superior to a subordinate. I was dumbfounded to hear his slant of this simple conversation. My husband explained that, by virtue of having been an officer in the Royal Swedish Air Force, his father was accustomed to grading the work of subordinates. My husband considered this as an affront against both of us, as an exhibit of inequity, placing me in some kind of class order as a servant.

The explanation was no more palatable than the engineered slight. It is also worthy to note that my husband had what I thought was a rather perverse sense of class distinction. Maybe it was because he had been a captain in the Swedish Merchant Marines, I don't know. I took away a sense of inferiority from my husband's comment. I think that a person in good emotional health would have told him to stuff it, or at least that I didn't agree with his view of things, or to confirm with him what he meant by his comments, and then forget it.

Instead, I not only accepted it, I internalized it. In fact, when my father-in-law died, I remember saying that I hated him for that backhanded compliment. What I didn't realize until much later was that my comments were part of my grieving. They were a kind of tear shed in anger and sadness, because I had the feeling that with the death of my in-laws, from whom my husband sought respect and acceptance, my world had changed forever. I didn't hate my father-in-law. I missed him and the sense of security and grounding I thought he gave to my husband.

I did something else when my father-in-law died. I took the silverware. I took the everyday silverware. I carried it with me in my suitcase so I wouldn't forget it. It never occurred to me that my stepson and his wife would have nothing to eat with during their stay at the folks' apartment. I just wanted life to be like it was. I wanted my husband to go on trying to please his parents. I pictured our family sharing a meal, as we had done so many times with my in-laws. I pictured this happening, now, in our own dining room in Washington, using the silverware and the dishes from my husband's Swedish family, a kind of tribute to them, a celebration of them, showing they remained with us in spirit. I wanted the silverware to still be used. I wanted life as I knew it to continue. I wanted to hold on. I just wanted to hold on. I guess I thought that in holding on, I could make my husband hold on too.

My ex-husband spent quite a bit of time and money filming his life, and our life together, our home and our family. Every year he would make at least one, and often two films that he would then have converted to PAL, the European network, so that my in-laws could have a VHS tape to enjoy the growth of their family. As long as my in-laws were alive, it seemed to me (though only mostly subconsciously I guess) that my husband was "on," he was performing; he was being the good son. He was an achiever. Now that his parents were dead, he no longer had anyone for whom to behave, no one he really had to please. He could express his anger. He could be the "bad boy." If you've never met someone like this, you won't have any idea what I'm talking about, and to you I say, "be thankful." For those of you who've met your own "bad boy," you know what I mean.

Part IV:
Tools of Realignment

My life had been thrown out of alignment. But, out of this time, I found some tools that are helping me to come to a place of balance. As R. Buckminster Fuller once said, "You never change things by fighting the existing reality. To change something, build a new model that makes the old one obsolete."

In fact, it was my attorney who gave me this idea. Not about changing, but about writing this book. During one of my consultations with him, I mentioned that I'd been reading every new age thing that I could get my hands on and following the recommendation of every person who talked to me. I wanted answers so badly. I wanted direction. I felt like a boat adrift in heavy seas. Where do I take my life now? In what direction? Where did I go wrong? Why was I so horrible?

When I saw the quote by R. Buckminster Fuller, I realized that what I'd been doing is just that, building a new system, changing my paradigm.

When I was growing up, I was taught to respect myself along with respecting others, but I don't recall being taught to honor myself. I think my mother had an inexhaustible reservoir of self-love or self-sacrifice connected to an "I am here to serve" mentality. This reservoir was replenished after little more than a night's sleep. It seemed like we were always doing something. We were helping make party favors for some community shindig, or cleaning up after some community shindig, or practicing for some community shindig. Or, we were driving to meet people to all go clamming or fishing or canning, or something. A Depression-era mother, there was always something to be done for someone else. I wonder how often this reservoir of self-love or self-sacrifice failed to be replenished. Perhaps it never failed her, and was continuously reserved for and by my mother. What I do know, though, is that I used to value myself not just because I was here on the planet, but by the activities and accomplishments that I could pack into the time that I spent here. I don't recall being instilled with a sense of freedom to just applaud and wonder at my own self.

How could she teach me something so foreign to herself? She seemed content with the idea that the more you sacrifice or do for others, the more it is okay to love yourself.

In other words, only by my deeds was I of value to myself. Oh, nothing earth shattering as a rule, like being a United States Senator while raising three children and writing hit plays, but just activities for my children, home, office, extended family, and friends. One weekend during a visit from my in-laws from Sweden, while I was in the middle of painting my daughter's bedroom after having put together a new furniture set my mother-in-law looked at me and asked me, "When do you relax?" It occurred to me then that this was one of the things that I truly admired about my mother-in-law, that she possessed the ability to enjoy life, that she felt no persistent necessity to put herself under stress.

At first I thought this attitude stemmed from having been taken care of for most of her life, as opposed to my own mother who took care of herself and others and had never, or so it seemed to me at the time, really had the luxury of being taken care of. My mother-in-law chose the job of a housewife, and she executed her job very well. Under closer examination, what I came to understand was that my mother-in-law had learned to honor and appreciate herself. She had learned to refill her own personal reservoir herself, not just from sleep, but from conscious daily effort of feeding herself in ways spiritually and culturally that honored her own personal values. It was a personal choice that she made. It was an executive decision. Neither of these women, my mother or mother-in-law, were better than the other for this choice. But, my mother-in-law was much healthier and lived longer. And, I think, she enjoyed a superior quality of life resulting from her conscious decision to value herself and to do what was necessary to honor herself.

So, I began to explore what the Italians call dolce far niente: how sweet to do nothing. I started to realize the importance of down time, of regrouping, of experiencing the moment and fully appreciating the experiences around me while they were happening. I began to try to value myself just because I am. Little by little, I stopped looking back at experiences for how I could have handled them differently and I began creating new experiences and paying attention to them. I made new friends, friends who valued themselves. I gave myself permission to spend my time in ways that made me feel joyful. Like they instruct us in the case of flight emergencies, I began the practice of putting on my own oxygen mask first. I cocooned, and I got to know myself better.

Like a turtle

*who carries her home
on her back,*

I am always at home.

NAL

Personal Space and Feng Shui

Psychologists will tell you that your house is often a metaphor for the self, and in my case I guarantee this was true. I suppose it's still true, but especially during this time of my life. I was allowing myself to explore my own self in a way that I hadn't done since I was a child, to really begin to rebirth myself. Every choice I made about my new space consciously directed my energy. When I moved into my apartment, I bought two things that were very special to me. Each made a statement that I now honored and valued myself, a reminder to myself and the universe that I am special every day and that I can make every day special: a set of 600 thread count Egyptian cotton sheets and a set of dishes by Spode in their Blue Italian pattern, to use every day.

    My apartment is in a Queen Anne-style home built in the Victorian era that was divided into six one-or-two-bedroom apartments. I found this place when I was driving by with my friend Linda. We were going to a ballet performance in Seattle and we'd gotten an early start in order to take a short drive through one of the more interesting areas of Tacoma, the Stadium District and Tacoma's North End. Lucky me, there was a sign on the lawn of this house saying there was a one-bedroom apartment for rent. When I phoned about it the next day, I was told it wouldn't be available for another month; Linda was kind enough to let me stay with her the remaining three weeks. The day I looked at the apartment, the owner of the building had a guest visiting at the same time. She mentioned to the guest that she preferred to have women renters: they were quieter and took better care of their space. She added that she was somehow always housing people who were homeless. I didn't, but I wanted to shout at her, "I have a home!"

    My apartment has one bedroom, a fireplace faced with marble and slate, hardwood floors throughout, and lovely little enhancements like a coffered ceiling in the large living room, corniced walls, and latticed windows. Both the basement, which houses a large old-fashioned laundry room, and my apartment have private entrances, while the other apartments share a large foyer and a beautiful stairway up to the second floor. There's a lovely lantern in the style of the early 1900s hanging inside the entry hall and another one on the front porch.

    The entrance to my apartment is through a carport and there's a patio and garden area just outside my front porch. The placement of my apartment, then, truly gives me this feeling of being in a safe cocoon. When I moved from my house in Lynnwood, I took only the bookcases and an overstuffed chair, which was the first new item of furniture I had ever purchased with my own money. Christmas was just around the corner and I envisioned my family sitting around my table for dinner on Christmas Eve; I envisioned my grandchildren, when grown, would remember the blue and white china that would be a signature in my household, hopefully adding to their sense of security, love, and family.

    Thank God for IKEA! I'd gone out to what was then the Fort Lewis Army base with my sister Sonja and picked up the electronics that I needed. I think I tired her out so much that day that when I started talking about what furniture I needed she just sort of glazed over and mentally raised her fingers in a gesture of "back, back you spawn of hell." She was, however, willing to schlep me over to IKEA to make purchases if that was what I desired. The purchases I'd made at the base were too large to fit into my car, so I drove home first and Sonja followed. While I waited for Sonja to arrive at my apartment, I started looking at the IKEA catalog. And, you know what I found? That's right: they deliver! I made a few notes, gave them a call, and within about ten minutes I'd spent some $2500. But, I had gained piece of mind. Fortunately for me, I had lots of experience putting furniture together. When I'd lived with my spouse in Lynnwood, it was always me who'd followed the directions and put together the various shelving units, beds, etc., that we'd purchased from IKEA and various stores anyway.

I took a vacation the day IKEA delivered my furniture. Oh, how exciting was this, my own stuff, with my own energy! I painstakingly put everything together: L-shaped sofa, dining room table and chairs. I'd chosen a damask blue sofa and the dining room chair cushions in a blue, tan and white striped pattern, since blue is the accent color for the bagua that is my living room/dining area. Later in this book, I go into more detail about my exposure and use of the art of placement called feng shui, where each area of one's home corresponds to a particular area of one's life for the purpose of the flow of energy: those areas are called baguas. In Feng Shui, there are nine baguas in a home. My living room happens to lie in the Feng Shui bagua that corresponds to knowledge and spirituality in my life, and also reflects mechanical objects such as cars.

Everything was in place for a Christmas that would radiate security, stability, a sense of family.

Later, I came to understand that one of the things I was doing at this time, aside from honoring myself in many ways, was trying to run away from the chaos I was feeling, to try instead to bring a normalcy to my life. In other words, I didn't allow myself to grieve at first. Many months later I finally began to acknowledge my grief and begin to really move forward on my own. My advice to anyone who goes through the end of a long-standing relationship: take your time to grieve, to be okay with the feelings that come up because they are all normal and natural, and we each have the capacity to learn and grow from our own feelings. We can trust ourselves, and we find a lot of that trust in the thoughts, feelings, and courage that find birth in the process of grieving.

After Christmas, I took myself shopping for a new bedstead. I'd bought a box spring and mattress from Macy's already during their pre-holiday sale, and I'd always wanted a four-poster. I went in to the Bassett store and leisurely went through the store in search for my dream bedroom suite. I was tired of cramming my clothes into the closet and one small dresser that I owned. So, I splurged. I bought a standing wardrobe for my clothes, a tall lingerie chest, a nightstand and then my beautiful four-poster bed--all in dark, solid, secure-feeling cherry. It was great fun and now, every time I'm in that bed, I feel so grateful to myself and to the universe.

The only thing I was really missing for my cocoon was a piano. For the first six months or so that I'd lived in my apartment, there was a beautiful old grand piano in the lobby. When that owner sold the property, she of course sold the piano as well. Unfortunately, I didn't have sufficient funds to make that purchase. I used to play that piano from time to time during the day. Then, I was lucky enough to find a digital grand piano at Costco for a price I could afford. I recall the day I bought it. I paid for the piano and then asked if there was perhaps some assistance for getting it to my place. No. Okay. Next, I called on my faithful resource, my sister Sonja, bless her heart. She gave me the phone number for a family friend and I called him up. "Sure," he said, "I'll pick it up tomorrow morning and bring it over." No amount of explanation on my part made it clear to him that this was a piano and not a keyboard. Despite my best efforts, he still seemed to envision this as a keyboard, maybe eighty pounds or so. Well, this instrument weighs about three hundred pounds when it's in the box. He worked it out, though, getting together a couple of his buddies to give him a hand and then one of them stayed and helped him follow the directions to put it together. I was never as overjoyed as when I was finally able to sit down, late into the evening, with my headphones on, and play to my heart's content.

All of the things I've placed in my environment evoke something wonderful for me. Whether it's a reminder that I am loved or reminders of where I'm headed—all of these things are symbols of a person and a life I love: me, and my life, just the way I am now.

Now I want to share a little about feng shui. This ancient art of orienting living spaces in an auspicious manner was the first way I learned to live life with intention. I had purpose in my life, yes, and goals, too. But feng shui supports your goals by enlivening your living space every day, through what you choose to pursue, for your intentions, in and for the various areas of your life. Previous to feng shui, I confess I lived my life largely in response to things around me. Even in my sales and customer service career, I was fulfilling someone else's goals and needs. Feng shui forced me to consider what I valued. So please, suspend any disbelief you may be feeling at the moment and walk a while with me into my world.

I've practiced feng shui since 1998. Feng shui is the art of placement in order to enhance the flow of chi, or life force, within your home. I was still in Lynnwood when I first heard about this art and I credit its practice with the fact that my former spouse and I sustained a relationship as long as we did. I was provided with training in the Black Hat Tantra school of feng shui and the main gist of this practice is to arrange the furnishings in your home to provide for the most beneficial flow of energy. When energy in the home is blocked, you may see a blockage in the corresponding area of your life.

Your home is comprised of nine baguas, each corresponding to nine areas of your life. Further, each room in your home is also comprised of nine baguas, each corresponding to and supporting, or conflicting with, an area of your life. The nine baguas are: family/past; wealth; health; helpful people; children/creativity; knowledge/spirituality; fame/success; career; and religion/spirituality.

In feng shui, any blockage in the chi, or life force, can be offset with a feng shui cure. There are mundane cures such as simply cleaning up the clutter or placing mirrors in strategic areas, and there are transcendental cures, which are often performed by a feng shui consultant. You can learn enough about feng shui to make it useful to yourself, especially if you are not financially able to afford a consultant.

As I've mentioned earlier, my living room happens to be in the bagua corresponding to knowledge and spirituality. The door of my living room, then, is a new bagua and the specific corner of my living room corresponding to knowledge and spirituality is the corner to the left of the door to the living room. As it happens, I have a tall bookcase in this area, packed with a variety of mundane as well as metaphysical books.

Now that you can picture my living room and understand the intentional placement within it, I'd like to detail the nine baguas. The order in which I present this listing is what one follows when blessing a home and it is called Tracing the Nine Stars. This is a sacred order designed to raise your intentions and purify your thoughts and wishes. You may find some of these techniques useful and wish to explore this subject further, in which case you will find helpful resources at the back of this book.

Family and Past

From the front door of your home, walk to the room or area located in the middle of the left side of your home. This is the area of your ancestors, but also your current family. In my apartment, this is a wall in my living room and to support my intentions in this area, I've placed the kilim that depicts the tree of life that my daughter brought me from the Middle East, a Renoir print of Dance at the Moulin de la Galette showing a joyful gathering, and a lush healthy plant. The intent of these articles is to lift the level of chi and to subconsciously remind me of the many gifts and talents that my family possesses, and for which I am so very grateful. I also have an old photo of my sisters and brother there in a green frame, because green is the color to enhance this bagua.

Wealth

From the front door of your home, walk to the room or area in the farthest left-hand corner. This is the area that speaks to your prosperity. This prosperity can be financial, spiritual, or fortunate blessings of any nature. This is an area in my apartment that is "missing," in other words there is no "room" per se, but only an area of a room. To bring this energy into my life, I've placed a mirror there that has been in my family for decades. It's a large mirror in a gilded wood frame and it magnifies, or brings into the room, the chi that may otherwise be missing or unusable to me. I also placed a lush philodendron there, whose green leaves symbolize increasing fortunate blessings. I keep this area free of clutter and I've also placed an intention where I see myself as being financially secure, with abundance flowing easily to me for the highest good of myself and others, and with my grateful thanks.

The enhancement colors for this bagua are black and purple. I have a purple glass jar in that corner where I do a daily Penny Dance. Every morning, I give thanks for the abundance I currently have in my life; and, for the loving and unlimited abundance that is coming to me. Pennies are used because they're still made with copper, and copper is used for conducting water and electricity. I took this from The Feng Shui of Abundance, A Practical and Spiritual Guide to Attracting Wealth into Your Life by Suzan Hilton. I like the way Suzan suggests the worldwide connection of copper in conducting currents. Acknowledging this in my morning practice seems to generate a wish for worldwide abundance.

Health

From the front door of your home, the health bagua is the room or area that lies directly in the center of your home. This is your health—the crux, as it were—of the wheel that is represented by your entire home, the balancing of all areas. I make sure to keep the area clear of clutter. Since yellow enhances the level of chi in the area of health, I've placed a glass painting depicting bright yellow calla lilies. This is above a little chest with a dark granite top where I have my keys, address book, and other articles that I reach for often during a normal day. This acts as a reminder to my subconscious that I choose balance and harmony in my daily life, and I gratefully acknowledge that I am supported by the universe with perfect health mentally, physically, spiritually, and emotionally.

Helpful People

Walk to the room that is to the far right of your front door, in the lower, far right corner of your home. That is the area of your home that works with the area of your life of helpful people and travel. In my case, that's my bedroom closet. Grey is the enhancement color for this bagua, and I've placed a few grey and white photos here as a reminder to myself that I have, and continue to attract into my life, an abundance of helpful people to help me with whatever I may need whenever I may need it. For these blessed people I am truly grateful. I always keep the closet neat and I often leave the door open during the day, to "let in" helpful people. The first time I did this, I was invited to the home of the people who own the house I live in for an art painting day. I don't paint often, or well, and the invitation was most unexpected. When I saw my easel sitting in the middle of my closet, with the open door, I wasn't quite so surprised.

I often have this door open and the light on to accent my willingness to accept help. My first voice-over job was, in fact, for a company in Toulouse, France, called Pinkanova. The job came out of the blue and I wondered how I'd gotten it. I still don't know, but I had to laugh when I next opened the closet to opportunity and saw my art pictures of Paris adorning the closet's walls where I had placed them because they're grey.

Children and Creativity

From your front door, walk to the right and to the room or area that is in the middle of the right side wall of your space or home. The flow of chi in this area corresponds to the creative aspects of your life, to your ability to dream and to manifest your dreams. The enhancement color for this area is white, so this is where I have my vision board/treasure map. It's just a blank picture covered in white flannel surrounded by a white frame. In it, I put pictures or other representations of what I'm manifesting. Now, of course, as you can imagine, as I write this, I have pictures of books and writers and joyful pictures of what represents healthy relationships to self and others. When I look at this, I am reminded of the variety of ways that I easily use my creative talents to benefit myself and the world, and the warm thanks with which I do so.

Knowledge and Spirituality

When you walk through your front door and turn to the left, this is the room or area that is at the far left from the doorway to your home. The chi in this room corresponds to knowledge of every kind, especially spirituality and self-knowledge. In my apartment, this is my living room. I have many blue articles in this room, since blue strengthens this area of my life; my intention for this area of my life is that I am constantly learning about myself and the world in fun and enjoyable ways. It also corresponds to mechanical objects, so if you've been experiencing a lot of car trouble or mechanical breakdowns, examine this area for clutter or broken objects and remove them.

I have bookshelves in every corner of this room filled with the books I love, so it's like having old friends continuously in this space. A fountain bubbles in one corner, cleaning the chi, the energy. Lush green plants peek from here and there and cut flowers sit atop the coffee table in a crystal vase. When times are lean, it's maybe only one flower, but it's still there. Above the fountain hangs a picture that I bought to benefit a fund for Guatemalan refugees. It's a block print on plain white paper depicting three women looking outward. They stand in a row with their arms intertwined. This represents, for me, an image of strength and empowerment, and also of community.

One wall is filled with framed pictures and artwork. A copy of an award I received, and a tribute to my uncle who was in the armed forces, family photos, a cubist painting by my daughter-in-law. A wedding photo of my son and his wife, photos of my grandparents, parents, siblings. I have a lot of family photos in the living room now and it feels wonderful having them around me, supporting me, loving me. This was a new experience for me, acknowledging the wonder of who I am and the wonderful people in my life; kind of standing with my peeps, so to speak.

Fame and Success

This is the room or area that is directly across from your front door, at the far end of your home. Its chi is enlivened and strengthened by the color red, and in my apartment this is my kitchen. I have my bright red KitchenAid mixer and coffee pot on one side, and on the other sits only a tall, thin bottle of flavored vinegar that has an arrangement of green and red chili peppers inside, a gift from my son and daughter-in-law at Christmas. The chi in this area corresponds to the way you are seen in the world. My personal intention for this bagua is to allow my light to shine in the world, to be loving, generous, and kind. I also place an intention here for the positive accomplishments that I make to my business environment and my community.

The refrigerator and stove occupy the left wall and I have a philodendron in a red pot growing on top of the refrigerator and hanging down in between the two, in order to ground the energy between the fire energy of the stove and the water energy of the refrigerator. On the right wall, in the creativity area of this bagua, sits a white microwave. One shelf above the sink displays a few of my cookbooks, and another set of philodendrons in bright red pots act as bookends. Because of its size and placement, I've needed to make several feng shui adjustments in this area. The stove, representing the various kinds of foods/energies that nurture your life and general prosperity, is very important to the energy flow of your life; consequently, you shouldn't have your back to the kitchen door when standing at the stove. In other words, no person (or by extension, nothing in life) can sneak up on you. My back is to the stove when I am cooking, so to remedy this I've added two corner shelves and on the bottom shelf I've placed a mirror. As an additional benefit, because it's in a wrought iron frame, I've been able to incorporate an additional balancing element of earth. I've also placed a mirror in a cute white frame above the sink, and tilted it so that I can see, from behind me, anyone who enters the kitchen. For the same reason, because my front door is directly across from my kitchen, I installed a lovely little chime on one of the pre-existing hooks hanging from the molding between the entryway and the kitchen.

These cures may have some practical aspects to them, but they are primarily intended to be symbolic.

Career and Life Path

This is the doorway of your home and the chi is strengthened by the color black. My front door is old and made of a nearly black wood with the top third enhanced with a leaded glass window. I make sure that this area is free from clutter and my intention surrounds my ability to easily attract, recognize, accept and maximize opportunities that enrich me and my employer, and to do so thankfully and joyously.

Relationships and Intimacy

The area of the home where you will find this bagua is, from your front door, to the right and in the farthest upper right corner from your doorway. This is the area where my bathroom is and because I want to enhance the chi in this area of my life, which is about relationships of every kind, I've placed a crystal in the center of the room. I've also left the walls the cheerful pink they were when I moved in, because pink is the enhancement color for this bagua. I've put a mirror on the outside of the bathroom door because it opens directly onto my bedroom and could, otherwise, disturb my sleep. Also, because this room has so much opportunity for the draining of energy, I've placed a brick in each of the four corners to symbolically keep my relationships grounded. The intention that I make for this area of my life has to do with all of the joyous and harmonious relationships that I choose to attract and maintain in my life. I am very thankful for all of these relationships.

There is an extremely helpful book by Nancy SantoPietro and Thomas Lin Yun Rinpoche called Feng Shui and Health: The Anatomy of a Home: Using Feng Shui to Disarm Illness, Accelerate Recovery, and Create Optimal Health. It's so practical because it has tons of cures for various health problems and other wonderful information.

During the process of my divorce, I didn't follow my own rules when it came to feng shui in the bedroom and although it may sound awfully weird to many readers, I seriously credit this for an increased lack of reality during this time. One rule in feng shui is that you need to place your bed, stove, and desk so that you are able to easily see the door and address any threat. This corresponds symbolically with your preparation in life so as not to be surprised. When I first moved in, I tried putting my bed against the appropriate wall. I kept waking up in the middle of the night, because I could hear the hot water heater going on and off in the basement, not to mention the rest of the house, through that bearing wall. So, I looked in my feng shui books for ideas for how to change the bed so that it would be against the wall with the door on it and still be protected; in other words, I wouldn't be able to see the door directly. I could do this by putting a mirror on the wall opposite the door. That's where my closet is. The only bad part about this was that my closet door had been painted so many times that it doesn't close properly. I was never able to actually line up the mirror on the outside of the door enough to see the bedroom door in its reflection. I noticed a big difference in my sense of personal empowerment, satisfaction, and self-trust when I changed the placement of my bed to see the door, once again, straight on while lying on my bed. By this time, I was more accustomed to the various sounds in the house, and the loud hot water heater had been replaced with a quieter, one. Unfortunately, I did this after my settlement conference and not before.

    I think it's kind of funny in a way. I remember when I first learned about feng shui from a woman who came to my home in Lynnwood. She walked through the house and then, when I opened the door to the clothes closet that I shared with my spouse, she said, "Oh, here you are!" The closet was filled with colorful hatboxes and colorful, uplifting posters. She said that, from the moment she'd walked in the door, the house felt so vanilla. Knowing me, she found this surprising. I hadn't given it much thought before then, but I'd actually shut a lot of myself away. My husband didn't ask me to shut myself away; he just didn't make it easy or comfortable when I was exploring my selfhood.

*I look into the mirror
and I scrunch up my eyes
and my nose,
and I pucker my lips,
and I say,
"I love you!"*

NAL

Physical self-care

I had used the house as a metaphor for myself, and now I moved on to the outer shell of my being. I was ready to begin to honor and value myself. I started by getting massages. Wow, what a great thing to do for yourself! At first, I went every week and then every two weeks. My daily drive to work, thirty-seven miles away, was about forty minutes with good traffic and an hour, to an hour and a half even, if there was an accident. All of that sitting really took its toll on my hamstring muscles. Combined with all the trauma of the violent incident locked inside those muscles, it took about five months of massage therapy to work through it all. My therapist said I was like concrete when I first came to her and, now I am very supple and relaxed.

    I recently read an article on the internet titled, "Marital Stress: Bad for a Woman's Heart." Researchers studied 279 females who were hospitalized after experiencing a heart attack. The results were significant. They found a three-fold higher risk than women with mild or no marital stress.

    I've always believed in the concept of anchoring myself in good health, since without that the rest of my plans falter. I started working out. My massage therapist was also a personal trainer and she helped me to develop a plan for myself that continues to work for me. I bought myself a weight bench and some free weights; I work out a couple of times a week. I have more stamina now and a better mood. I also take vitamins and watch what I eat and drink.

    One of the nicest things that my family forced me to do is to go to a spa. Imagine. Time invested in you alone. For no other reason than because it's fun and relaxing. And, it's rejuvenating. My daughter and daughter-in-law took me the first time, as a treat. We have a Korean women's spa here in Tacoma, and they have another one up in Lynnwood that opened up right after I moved down here. Allow me to elaborate, for anyone who is curious about the spa experience.

This may be old hat to many people, but it wasn't to me and I'm willing to bet that it's foreign territory to a lot of women.

The Olympus Women's Health Spa is open from a.m. to p.m. Monday through Thursday, and they are open on Friday and Saturday from a.m. to a.m., isn't that gorgeous? So, you can go after work if you feel like it. They are closed on Sunday. I have to admit that, often, Sunday is the most convenient day for me to go. But, I've taken to going on Saturdays too.

When you walk in, you're met by a woman, or two or three, sitting or standing behind an L-shaped black marble counter. They greet you warmly and ask if you've been there before or not. If it's your first visit, the tour is free, and you needn't go in on that day if you don't feel like it. But, I guarantee you should.

You pay for the services you want that day. The initial entry fee is $30.00 and that entitles you to use the baths and heated rooms. In addition, you can select a massage, a cleansing scrub, a moisturizing scrub, a body wrap, or several other services. You're handed a bundle and a locker key that is attached to a vinyl-wrapped elastic bracelet and has the number of your locker. The bundle holds a bath towel, a hand/face towel and a thin white cotton robe so soft you know it's been washed many thousands of times.

The layout is much like a private home and there are bathrooms scattered throughout. There is nothing institutional about the place. When you walk through the front door, you are filled with a sense of peace and security, totally safe from the outside world. Take off your shoes and place them in the cubby that has your locker number and then walk through to something that looks like a living room. You'll see overstuffed sofas and chairs, thick wall-to-wall carpeting and a mural of the sea depicting a scene one might gaze at through the open patio from inside a Grecian or Roman spa. You'll find small touches of artwork, silk flowers and baskets and sachets of charcoal and potpourri accenting the rooms.

Move to your locker, set in a dormitory-style dressing area that is complete with Q-tips, Kleenex, lotions, water cooler, and scale, as well as hair combs and brushes maintained by an ultraviolet cleaner. Clothes safely stowed in your locker, you'll don the cotton robe. Feel how soft it is near your skin. The temperature is very pleasant and you feel almost as though you are in a dream. Especially after the first time, there is something very special about even putting on the robe. Your body knows what's coming, knows this is safe and relaxing and purely exquisite.

You open the door into the baths. Before you is a room made of heated marble and tile. You put your robe in the cubby corresponding to your locker number. Now, shower off and then enter the mineral bath where the soothing 93 degree temperature and the intimate size fits just you, or maybe you and two other people if you feel like chatting. Then, try the 90 degree Jacuzzi, or the 97 degree Jacuzzi tub and the 104 degree Jacuzzi. Often you will meet new people or see old friends. If you feel like it, you can chat, or, if you want to be alone, you can find solitude as well.

Ready for a change of pace, you move to the wet sauna to give your lungs a nice refreshing cleanse to open the pores and release the toxins that have been making your muscles ache. Then, maybe you will want to dip into the cooling pool and splash under the waterfall, maybe into the dry sauna.

I like to make several trips of this, staying about ten minutes or so in the saunas at any one time. There's a narrow pool filled with warm water steeped with mugwort. Mugwort is an herb known to assist your body in releasing toxins through sweat and dowsing with several pans full of mugwort makes for a nice transition from the cold bath back into the sauna, or at any point in the process.

You will also want to try the infrared saunas. I had never been in an infrared sauna, and I was so in for a treat. Each room has a basket of charcoal to neutralize odors. While lying on the soft cotton blanket of the floor of the salt room, it seems like you can taste the salt underneath as your body absorbs it. The snowflake design of the pillow covers in the Sand Room along with the river rock on the walls in shades of grey and blue add to a peaceful ambiance. And, the 160–170 degrees of the Mud and Jade Room, with its carpet of birch wood, makes it pleasant to sweat profusely and sweetly send the toxins out of your body. Be sure to drink a lot of water and stay no more than thirty minutes at one time in these rooms.

To take a break and be sure that you're well nourished, you will want to visit the restaurant. There are several vegetarian dishes, but I usually get the spicy barbeque pork. This is very spicy and ignites the fire of my soul and the shining spark of my intellect. The slender but stocky Korean lady smiles gently as she brings my meal. Seven small bowls the size of a fruit dish are laid down first and the eighth dish is the entree. The side dishes vary, but are usually a slice of steamed tofu marinated in a mild soy sauce and sweet chili sauce; spinach that has been steamed briefly in water filled with sea salt and on which still hangs the flavor of the sea, garnished with a pinch of toasted sesame seeds; fermented black beans; angular chunks of steamed potato and carrot swimming in a feathery sea of honey, peanut oil and garnished with green onion; steamed mung bean sprouts; lightly steamed zucchini and onion topped with a light sesame oil; a mild kimchi; lastly, pickled daikon radish. The pork glistens in a light and spicy sauce with sliced yellow onion, large pieces of green onion, and sliced cabbage.

I'll bet that Korean people never have colds because nothing could grow in this vinegary and spicy environment. What a delightful juxtaposition of foods—the combination of textures and colors, of hot and sweet. Music! Music to your mouth. Positively orgasmic! Roasted corn tea, included in the price of the meal, is earthy and balancing.

I try to get a full body renewal once every quarter, and I try to get to the spa at least once a month. For a full day of body renewal, that means at least five hours. It's wonderful! Five hours all on YOU. Start with a leisurely breakfast at home and then over to the spa for a good soak to help relax before a heavenly massage for sixty or ninety minutes. This gets your muscles nice and supple. Then, to clear the toxins and rejuvenate your skin, here comes a small, thin lady with muscular upper arms. She leads you through a passageway and directs you to lie face down on a vinyl covered massage table. She asks, "Are you allergic to anything?" "No." Now just lie back while she scrubs your skin. She puts a cloth on each hand that resembles a fine grit of sand paper and then she scrubs your whole body with flat hands and a back and forth motion as though she were walking. Then, she takes a piece of plastic cloth and lathers it up with a fresh-smelling cucumber soap and scrubs your whole body with it. Then, you turn over and she does it all over again. This cleansing massage takes about an hour. Then, you go have lunch or back to the baths, or the saunas and go back for a moisturizing scrub. Picture oil, and honey, and aloe. You exit the spa feeling renewed and refreshed, looking like you could conquer the world and feeling like it too.

    Not only are you pampering yourself and reminding yourself how wonderful and special you are, you're also washing away toxins, including emotions and ideas that have become outdated and don't serve you anymore. When I can't afford to have the entire cleansing experience performed by the professional staff at the spa, on my monthly visits I at least do the scrub myself. The spa sells the scrubbing cloths and the soaps, etc. I keep my spa supplies in the trunk of my car in case I want to pop in there right after work.

    At home, I have another set of the scrubbing cloths in the bathroom. Here, I need to get a little more creative in order to get the toxin-freeing effect. I put in two cups of Epsom salts and either a half cup of sea salt or a half cup of baking soda (sea salt for toxins and baking soda for effects of electromagnetic fields, also known as EMFs). I use the hottest water I can handle and I put on my timer for twenty minutes. Sometimes it's difficult to stay in the water that long, but it's worth it. I try to let my mind wander to places I want to go and experiences I want to have, and the crazier the better. I have one of those old claw-footed bathtubs deep enough to emerge my five foot two inch frame within. If you can't fit all the way in because of your bathtub's design, try putting hot washcloths over the exposed parts to get the sweat going.

Once I've immersed my skin in the hot water for at least twenty minutes, I take my scrubbing glove and work it over my skin. Sometimes at this point I need to get out of the water for just a few seconds to drink some cool water or get a breath of air. The thoroughness of this step is really important to me. Okay, I know this sounds super gross, but you can see the dead skin just peel off in huge flakes sometimes. At the spa, you can get rid of the water easily and refresh it, but at home of course you're just lying in it, around and under this layer of disgusting sludge. It's all in how you look at it, though. I like to see bunches of sludge in the water because that way I know I'm doing a really good job.

The second step is to go over the skin once again, but this time with the other tool, the plastic cloth. I get this as soapy as I can and then I go over every inch of my body one more time. Now, I'm ready to shower off all of the dead skin and wash down the bathtub.

Out of the tub now, I need to get some good quality moisture back into my skin. Since I'm older, my skin tends to be dry; I use a good hospital grade lotion, like Lubriderm, all over my body. The whole process takes about an hour and it feels wonderful to dispel those toxins.

*To see your best self
reflected back at you
in the eyes of another ...
ah, that is
magnificence*

NAL

Energy Work

From my massage therapist, I was led to an energy worker by the name of Dale Gordon. Dale practices out of her home, which is in Tacoma's North End neighborhood. It, like my apartment house, is a Queen Anne-style home from the Victorian era, huge and imposing. The home itself is set back from the street on a large, beautifully landscaped lot with full junipers and cypress, huge, leafy rhododendrons, a small pond, and a winding stream. The house has a large formal entry hall where side doors lead to other parts of the house and a giant staircase seems to carry the happy shadows of countless hopeful brides. In fact, Dale explained to me that yes, there had been hundreds of weddings in that home.

    Dale herself was very sweet in appearance. Standing about 5'8" and very thin, she wore comfortable soft looking beige pants and a form fitting top. Her graying blonde hair was shoulder length and her slender face was accented by large rimless eyeglasses.

    Dale led me upstairs to a bedroom in the corner of the house with a view of Commencement Bay out of two of the windows. There was a bookshelf full of old books and on top were several bells of different sizes, most of them pretty large ones, up to ten and twelve inches in diameter. A comfortable massage therapy table sat in the center of the room and two comfortable Victorian chairs sat in front of the window.

    Dale explained to me she had been a behavioral psychologist and after spending a lot of time in the Southwestern United States and abroad, she had learned several techniques for healing people by breaking through their blocked chakras. She explained to me how this was like psychotherapy, only much quicker. She began our session by telling me that, during her meditation about me earlier that day, she had pulled out a rune stone and an animal card. The rune stone represented transition. I don't remember the animal card, perhaps because that was my first exposure to animal cards,

cards that depict animals as totems/messengers. After that, we talked for half an hour or so and then I laid down on the massage table. Dale went through a short series of questions regarding what behavior was acceptable to me. She uses scents and bells; sometimes touches the seat of the chakra, and she needed to know if any of these were unacceptable to me.

I could talk or not during the session, it was up to me; my eyes could be open or closed, also up to me. I kept my eyes closed for the most part. Dale moved her hands over my body, from feet to head, usually a few inches above my body. She used a wonderful, primordial scent. I think the bells were in the tone of C and D. I started to cry, it was such a release. It was like a dam had broken. It was wonderful.

We were able to unblock all but my fifth chakra. For that, I needed a second session. I'd been having fifth chakra issues like Temporomandibular joint disorder (TMJ) and thyroid problems in particular, for some time. This chakra also deals with the "authentic self." I had negotiated away a lot of my authentic self, buried it so deeply within my psyche as I gave away more and more to a variety of survival issues. Afterward, I asked Dale what she did to renew her own energy after these sessions. She replied, "I don't use my energy. I use your energy. I don't do anything at all; I'm only a conduit, a tool."

Dale reminded me that, similar to massage therapy, chakra therapy works from the inside and breaks up dead cells so it's important to drink a lot of water to flush the dead cells out of my body after this session.

During the first part of our meeting, Dale suggested that I read Goddesses in Older Women: Archetypes in Women Over Fifty by Jean Shinoda Bolen. She also asked if I was journaling and I said, "Sporadically." In fact, extremely sporadically. She suggested two other books that might be helpful: Visual Journaling: Going Deeper than Words by Barbara Ganim and Susan Fox, and SoulCollage® by Seena B. Frost. Visual Journaling and SoulCollage® are programs designed to tune in to your right brain through pictures that your left brain interprets. The left brain is verbal and has a very short memory; the right brain is pictorial and stores everything, including scent and taste sensations.

I have not had to truly think of myself, for myself, for years. There was always some task to perform, someone to care for. Goddesses in Older Women is designed to help one tap into the archetypal energies of the crone stage of life, the older woman. It's delightful and I highly recommend it.

*And it came to pass
that the little girl grew into a
wonderful woman who gave
away so much love and
kindness that,
though years passed and
passed,
those who could receive her
gifts
saw not one wrinkle
in her countenance*

NAL

Visual Journaling

When my daughter lived at home, we would often shop at Daniel Smith Artists' Materials in Seattle. We used to spend a lot of time and money there. When my son was growing up, I wasn't able to indulge many of his creative wishes and with my daughter I wanted it to be different. I wanted her to experience herself in all of the many ways that surfaced and wanted to be voiced. She explored stamp making, linoleum art, pottery, sculpting, watercolors, oils, pastels, practically every medium. This time, it was all for me! It was so exciting; I felt like a kid. This was for my psyche, my inner world and my inner work. Just taking that first step was so scary and, yet, such a turning point, showing respect for my own inner voices wanting to emerge. It's been slow going, I tell you. I've been trapped inside for so long, from my own choices.

In Visual Journaling, you first bring yourself to a relaxed emotional state, either by using music or movement. Then, you either draw or paint a picture, whatever seems to suit your soul at the time. You don't need to use any elaborate materials. If you don't have paints or markers around, use crayons. It doesn't matter what the medium is, and you don't have to invest a lot of time in the activity. Don't let a tight schedule get in the way of this bit of self-exploration. The next step is to sit back and interpret your piece. I think that this practice becomes more effective when used regularly.

I had a lot of resistance to this at first. Still, it is fascinating, getting to know myself. I'm sure everyone finds themselves fascinating when they actually pay attention to the thoughts and feelings in their imaginations and in their very cells. This is no time for anything disciplined. This is working from your soul. What's on your mind today? You begin by asking a question, similar to tarot, or you can go through the process without it. I've discovered a lot of anger, and also a lot of potential and self-confidence. This is a process that can give voice to your soul. I turned off the television, just for a while, and turned on my inner vision.

*Lucky is the woman
who seeks her best self every
day
and sleeps well every night
having found her*

NAL

SoulCollage®

One of the most interesting things I've studied is a practice that's done with reading and interpreting cards. The name and information in the practice is proprietary and, because of the time involved in permissions for using the copyrighted name, I prefer to just talk about my experience. If you want to pursue it further, you can visit the website that's in the back of this book, or you can contact me with questions or to get a group going. I was so fascinated by this practice that I became a certified facilitator.

I first read about the concept of making your own cards and then doing readings from them when I went to see Dale Golden. Dale told me about the book and I immediately took her advice and sent for a copy. I think I had to order it directly from the publisher, Hanford Mead, but I don't recall for certain. I excitedly ordered a stack of the special pre-cut cards, each about an eighth of an inch thick and measuring five by eight inches. I even went out and bought special decorative paper for the backs of the four different suits.

This concept seems, basically, to be about giving voice to your right brain. Your left brain is the side that speaks and your right brain, which holds all of your memories (even those from past lives, some say), has no voice and speaks only in images. The book I read was SoulCollage®, an Intuitive Collage Process for Individuals and Groups, by Seena B. Frost. Since then, this book has gone out of print and has been replaced by a new one entitled SoulCollage® Evolving. You begin by randomly taking images from magazines or other sources that suit you. You can also use old photographs.

I started making my cards at the Paradise Inn. I had collected magazines and torn out pictures, but it took a while to find things interesting enough to actually use in my cards. I really resisted this process at first. I think one of the reasons is that it makes me accountable. I am responsible for my life, for my tomorrows, by the actions I take, or the actions I choose not to take, today. At my age, I have made a lot of choices and sometimes I only see the bad ones. This process is about accessing my own intuition to assist me now. That seemed very empowering to me; and, as I've said, it also seemed a little scary.

Paradise Inn on Mount Rainier was soon to close for renovations and would not reopen for another two years. I arrived at the park on August 29th. I could have waited a week or so until after Labor Day when there would be fewer children racing about, but I really needed a break from work and my routine right then. I still had a lengthy commute to and from work and it made for a very long day. Upon entering my room, which was quite small, I suddenly was reminded of a very uncomfortable memory concerning my husband and daughter and a time when I had been less than pleasant. I nearly bolted. Then I decided the room would look more appealing once I had my own belongings around me. I often travel with a photo of my family now, just for these moments, to make a place my own. I don't recall if I had one at that time or not, but nonetheless I committed myself to my little holiday and told myself to just buck up.

The inn was very cozy; I was curious what they could do to it with the renovation. There were these lampshades all over the common area of the inn. I'd seen them before on lamps at Lake Quinault, where I spent much of my summers until I was well into high school. They're an American Indian design. I think they're made of some kind of parchment paper, with local flowers pressed into them and shrubbery hand painted around them. I did a lot of walking. I probably could have done more, but I allowed myself to become frightened when I got too far away from other people.

I did some painting while up there as well. Everyone on the trail stopped to take a look. It was a little embarrassing because I am a lousy painter. Well, let's just say I am a very inexperienced painter. Mothers called their children "Oh look, dears, there's an artist at work." I'm serious, this was an actual comment. Artist? I can hardly draw a straight line, and I'm sure I cannot manage to give that straight line any depth. Anyway, one bunch was from Gothenburg, Sweden. Spare me. I was not the least interested at that time in meeting anyone I thought may even remotely know my husband or any member of his friends or family.

    Well, back to the cards. The SoulCollage® book suggests four suits. One suit represents your inner committee, the parts of you that you share with the world, and the beliefs that direct you. This could be the worker, the speaker, the judgmental bitch, the inner child, the happy camper, the inner director, or the observer, as examples. The second suit of cards represents your community, to bring in their positive energies. This is the suit where you don't want anything or anyone you consider toxic. You may include photos or drawings of local landmarks as well, and pets. The third suit, the companion suit, represents the physical energies of your body and is reserved for animals who present themselves while you meditate on the seven chakras. The fourth suit is the council suit, and it represents archetypal energies of which examples are the saboteur or the prostitute, the fairy queen, or goddess. At the risk of poorly discussing the particular book, I want to just tell you about my experience with it. In answering the various questions that were asked in the book, I realize, again and still, that I didn't want to be around people. It was as though my togetherness gene was all screwed up. I didn't want to be around anyone for very long. I just wanted to cocoon. I just wanted to grieve. Now, as I move through this third edition, there are so many people in my life who are fun to be with on so many different levels, and I feel so lucky to have come through that other time of isolation. I have been told you can find wonder and joy in others only after you have found the wonder and joy in yourself. I agree with that statement.

    My experience with the suit about the chakra animals was the most difficult for me. If you have never worked with chakras, or find it hard to make time to meditate, you can omit this suit. But, if you persevere, I think you'll find a depth of energy and a perception that is unique. The animals pick you, you don't pick the animals. Originally, I made the squirrel my animal for my first chakra, the survival chakra, choosing to gather all the precious nuts who are my family and friends and to gather the kernels of truth I've come to know from them, shoring myself up for any possible future winter of the soul. But, then I read the book again, and followed the author's meditation. I'm still working with this one. If you have animals in your life, I think this will probably be easier for you.

Many of you know about chakras and work with them. For those who may be unfamiliar with this, though, I'll list the chakras briefly. The first chakra is your survival or root chakra and sits in your pelvic area and down through your legs and feet. The second chakra houses your creativity, it's your social chakra, and it sits just below your navel. The third chakra houses your personal power, your will. It sits near your solar plexus. The fourth chakra is your heart chakra, just behind the heart. The fifth chakra is the seat of your creative self-expression, your authenticity, and it resides in your throat. The sixth chakra houses your intuition and is the point on your forehead just between your eyes. Lastly, the seventh chakra, known as your transpersonal chakra, is above your head. Chakras are said to be our internal energy systems. There are many books on the subject. Anatomy of the Spirit: the Seven Stages of Power and Healing by Caroline Myss, Ph.D., is an excellent reference when beginning work with chakras.

One of the cards I made is called Respect. It shows lines of people from different lands, and when I gave voice to that card, what I came up was something to this effect: "I Am One Who wants to be seen for myself and not part of a crowd. I want your respect but I have not given you all the tools to feel that." It's quite a profound little card, filled with pinks and reds, and a wonderful reminder to me of the value of all cultures and my good fortune to be able to interact with them, for I believe we truly are all one.

After making these cards, you read from them. This is best done in a group. In fact, the entire process is best done in a group. If you have, say, three people, one can be the card reader; the next one can write what the card reader says; and then the third person facilitates, tasked with holding a safe and sacred space.

There is more to this process, but what I've gotten from it is, primarily I think, validation. My feelings and my thoughts, they are all valid and do not require the interpretation of a third party. I am wise, when I listen to myself. I possess wisdom. This process is a concrete practice to answer my questions and it can be very effective in prompting a change in perspective.

Light the fire
that burns in the temple of my soul.
Pump the bellows
as I sit idly by.
I want to breathe.
Breathe, breathe, breathe
to transit—beyond the wanting—and arrive once again
at the birth
of our immortal soul

NAL

Intuitive Counseling

I think I learned about Dorothy Lynn from my massage therapist too. Dorothy Lynn has been in social work and intuitive healing for over thirty years; her office is in Freight House Square in Tacoma. I've seen her for two sessions, several months apart. I believe in reincarnation; I've always thought of myself as an old soul, mostly because so many people I see on the street look familiar to me, as though I've seen them before somewhere. Dorothy Lynn was able to tell me about two previous lives in which I had interacted with my ex-husband. In one past life, I had been his slave. In another lifetime, I had been his son. Abandoned for the sea when I was first born, he returned for me when I was a teenager and took me against the wishes of my mother onboard his ship. An angry man, he one day took out his anger on me and I jumped overboard, leaving my father to think I was dead.

The most important part of this equation, of course, is that she could tell me how I could make it less likely that I would see him in another lifetime. One of the things she told me was to make a list of anything that he had ever done to me, all of the things that I could think of, every slight, every humiliation, everything, and do this over the period of several days. Then, once this process felt complete, no matter how long it took, take the list and burn it. The third part of this process is, once those thoughts surface, deflect them by picturing in your mind that burned piece of paper. You needn't deal with this any longer, since you already did: you burned it up and it is gone. End of story.

Flowers--fresh flowers. Dorothy Lynn assisted me with a lot of chakra therapy and deprogramming, at which she seems to be expert. As part of expressing to yourself how wonderful and worthwhile you are, give yourself fresh flowers and treats. They don't need to cost a lot. Sometimes, I've only had one rose in a bud vase on my desk, or on my dining table. Other times, it's been a few tulips, and sometimes even large bouquets.

Costco has a lot of good deals on flowers, and even my local Thriftway has good deals on different flowers. Every time I look at those flowers, that's an opportunity to tell myself how much I love me and how grateful I am that I've shown up on this planet at this time.

    Dorothy Lynn also reminded me that I could call on the angels at any time for assistance. Rafael and Uriel have become my two favorites. She also told me about Paramahansa Yogananda, the first great master of India to live in the West for any length of time. I remember being exposed to him, only by seeing his face, when I was young, but I knew nothing about him. She suggested I might read his book, Autobiography of a Yogi, which I did. As I grow more secure, I call on him more and more for bits of guidance in any number of situations both large and small.

I find that
I magnify that on which I dwell.
I am thankful for
my health, my family, my neighbors,
my colleagues,
for clean water, clean air,
and peace
in my world|
now.

NAL

Meditation

In the past, I was not one to meditate, per se. Meditating can be done while gardening, cooking or baking, knitting or crocheting. I did those things, but when Dorothy Lynn suggested I might try mediation, I took advantage of the opportunity to explore something new. She made a meditation tape for me to start with. Since then, I've gotten a few other CDs, and some of the other books I've been reading have some meditations that I've recorded for myself. I've toyed with the idea of going to a mediation retreat, but I've not taken advantage of those yet. I do find meditation to be very calming and empowering. Even if it's only ten or fifteen minutes, it makes for a great start to the day, as well as a good way to stay centered during the day, and a pleasant way to wind down in the evening. Sometimes I can just meditate for ten minutes or so, and other times an hour is just right. It just depends on how I feel. I honor myself, whatever the choice.

*Show me the way to
happiness, joy, and laughter,
I said to my guardian angel
in a dream this morning.
With her ethereal arm,
she pointed to my heart and
replied,
"It is right there, within you."*

NAL

Healing through Archetypes and Chakras

I've found the writings of Caroline Myss very helpful because she talks about the reasons why we are here. From my initial exposure to Ms. Myss through her book Anatomy of the Spirit, I progressed to Sacred Contracts. The premise of Ms. Myss is that we each have twelve archetypes at work in our lives.

Though I tried in the previous section, this word archetype is a difficult concept to explain, I think. The dictionary defines it as a prototype. An archetype is an energy that has evolved through millennia as an energy all humanity has in common, although we may have different thoughts about our own personal interaction with that archetype depending on our background and values. For example, you may think of "prostitute" and envision a tall thin woman in a short tight skirt; someone else may envision an attorney, or a salesperson. No matter what image you see, this title evokes some kind of image in each of us. Ms. Myss suggests that, man or woman, the four archetypes basic to each of us, in some form are: the Inner Child, the Victim, the Prostitute, and the Saboteur. Her feeling is that these four archetypes "...symbolize our major life challenges and how we choose to survive. Together they represent the issues, fears, and vulnerabilities that cause us to negotiate away the power of our spirits within our physical world." Besides these four, we have eight others that come and go in our lives. Everyone is different and will have eight different archetypes that come and go in their lives. Typical of these eight, however, are the Healer, the Rescuer, the Servant, the Mystic, the Visionary, the Knight, the Pioneer, and the Prince. For this part of the process, Ms. Myss suggests you select eight primary and three secondary archetypal companions.

During my reading of this book, I wanted to honor this process and so I decided to put my archetypes explorations into a special book. There's a delightful gift shop in the Proctor District of Tacoma called Giardini Gift and Garden. They stock Portmeirion porcelain, porcelain dolls, clothing, books, and stationary from France and Spain. This is a place I would have considered before as being too tempting, somewhere I likely would have stayed away from, or moved through quickly, because of how I thought of money, and of myself, and of my own value.

I selected a blank book with a spiral binding and a cover long enough to write on either side of the page and still have a firm foundation. I took this blank book with me as well as the soul collage stuff for my long weekend at Mount Rainier's Paradise Inn. That was one of the best things I've ever done for myself!

Ms. Myss suggests that you ask those archetypal energies within yourself a series of questions. I began this exercise with the inner child and, as Ms. Myss suggested, I wrote the questions with my right hand and then I wrote the answers in another color ink. I chose pink for my non-dominant hand, the left hand in my case. On the following pages are the answers to those first questions as I wrote them in my book.

Historical questions:

1. Why did I choose you?

Answer: To get to know me.

2. Where have we met before?

Answer: When we lived with Mom; when we played with children. When we watched Alexis have things we wanted; hen we see Kylin seeming to write effortlessly.

3. How does your shadow self influence me?

Answer: I am impatient.

4. What do I like least about you?

Answer: I'm hard to control, to discipline.

5. Which opportunities in my life are connected to your energy?

Answer: All the good ones.

Personal questions:

1. Who are you most connected to in my life and how has this connection contributed to our spiritual development?

Answer: Jan (my ex-husband) protects me. I know that you can protect me now. I'm connected to Rosalie and Sonja (my sisters). They have loved me and freed me to explore.

2. How do you help me fulfill my contracts with other people?

Answer: I make you joyful so you can do things with a smile.

3. Who in my life do I associate with your power?

Answer: Daniel (my grandson) and Lars (my son).

4. Who are you connected with from my past that I have unfinished business with? In what way can your influence bring closure to each of these relationships?

Answer: That old lady, Marge Smith, who was so manipulative and hurt my feelings. Ron (my brother, deceased) maybe. You can protect me. You can tell people when they hurt my feelings or when they don't pay attention to me.

Energy and Intuitive Questions

1. How do I know when your energy is influencing my thoughts and actions?

Answer: We feel left out. We feel happy or sad.

2. How do you present your energy to me through the dream state?

Answer: When we fly and when we have a lot of clothes.

3. In what ways does your influence enhance my personal power?

Answer: In every way, I think. I help you to be strong. I help you to be light and joyful so you can be happy and help other people be happy. They just can't resist us.

4. Do you have a negative influence on my behavior or attitudes?

Answer: Sometimes I can make you spend more money. But, really, no, nothing negative.

5. What have I learned lately that comes directly from you?

Answer: How to listen to me. How to have fun.

6. When and where in my life have you communicated with me most directly?

Answer: When we left Lynnwood. When you had to protect me. When we came home from Florida, I think.

7. What do you make me afraid of? Name at least five things.

Answer: people (some people); singing; talking; getting to know people, unless they want to play; speaking to groups; the dark;

walking in the dark; swimming in lakes (ooky things around my feet).

8. What positive characteristics do I have that you enhance and help me with? Name at least five.

Answer: you're strong; you're willing to try new things; you try hard to make good things; you help people; you have a good imagination.

9. As a child, I imagined being a king, a queen, a slave, a warrior, princess, a femme fatal. What is your contribution to my spiritual development?

Answer: I help you to ask a lot of questions. (This one I found very curious because sometimes I won't ask questions...could this be when I am not allowing my inner child a voice?)

10. What are the most important personal lessons that you have taught me?

Answer: When we were approached by Dave Hoag (a relative who tried to molest me when I was young) I taught you how to speak up, to be brave, to be a tattletale in a good way. I taught you how to listen.

11. What immediate guidance can you give me in this present moment?

Answer: Be strong and keep listening to us and protecting us.

12. How do you help me work with my agreements and contracts?

Answer: I want to respect you, so I guess I help you to keep your agreements, to honor your contracts. I tell you if something scares me or if it feels bad or wrong.

13. What is the most immediate personal change connected to your influence that I can make that would best empower me at this point in my life?

Answer: Have more fun and get more exercise. Play a lot more. Make believe a lot.

14. How do you cause me to block personal change?

Answer: I don't think I do cause that. Go for it. Change. I guess if it's something that's not fun anymore like really boring stuff, then I don't help you. Like, a lot of studying or really, really uncomfortable stuff for a long time, that's hard to support.

15. What do I fear most about your influence?

Answer: That I'll make you so happy you won't want to act like a grownup. You'll want to play all the time. You're afraid we'll say something stupid or cruel.

From this exercise, I learned that my inner child is fun and creative, innocent and happy, and absolutely insistent on having attention.

*I,
Nadine,
now
act from
my authentic self.*

NAL

Affirmations

I'd used affirmations for many years for a variety of things, but mostly for making practical adjustments to my life or self. I took a class on it once, a long time ago, and I found it quite fascinating and helpful. It's a technique that's served me well. When making affirmations, they need to be claimed in the present moment, be believable and able to be believed by the subconscious (not necessarily the same as realistic, since it depends on the strength of one's imagination); and, they need to be personal. Apparently the subconscious is very literal. I've used affirmations to increase my earnings. The books I've read suggest setting a goal for increasing earnings that is one and a half to two times what you're earning now. I might say, "I, Nadine, now earn at least $200,000.00 in 2010." One affirmation I used while still married was, "I, Nadine, am now an excellent listener and I wait my turn before speaking." And, "I, Nadine, am now an excellent money manager." It's personal. It's in the present. It's believable.

Have you read You Can Heal Your Life by Louise L. Hay? Anything that Hay House, her publishing company, puts out is wonderful. I fell upon You Can Heal Your Life at a used book store when I first moved to my little apartment and I absorbed every word like it was an aspirin.

I had some psoriasis and I noticed the other day that it's nearly gone. There is just a very light pink coloring where once there was a large patch of bright red. Here is what Ms. Hay has to say about the causes of psoriasis in her book: "Fear of being hurt; deadening the senses of the self; refusing to accept responsibility for our own feelings." Man, was that me. Part of being responsible for your feelings is that you stick up for them, you defend them, and set boundaries with people. Now, I could do that in a vacuum just fine, and I could do that at work and with my children, but with my husband? That was a tough one.

My sinus problems have also lessened. Louise says sinus problems are caused by "Irritation to one person, someone close." I'm sure I had allowed myself to become very irritated with my spouse, and with myself for patterns I had either engendered or allowed to be sustained in that relationship. Louise's antidote is to repeat this affirmation: "I declare peace and harmony indwell me and surround me at all times. All is well."

Another thing I got rid of was bad breath. Ooh, don't you just hate that? I used to have horribly bad breath. Here's what Louise says about the causes of bad breath: "Anger and revenge thoughts, experiences backing up." Well, that was me, in many ways.

I still have survival issues, and anger issues, lots of them, and they show up in different parts of my body. Doesn't everyone have various kinds of survival and anger issues that they're working through at different times? I think this is normal and will never really go away, and that's okay. It's part of life and I think it's probably good for us. Acknowledging and addressing issues as they present themselves in interactions with those we love—that, I think, is the key to life and growth. That's how you show up for your life and set boundaries, by respecting yourself first and then extending that same respect to others. But, it has to be felt for ourselves first. I repeat the affirmations prescribed by Ms. Hay. They work well. I repeat to myself: "The past is forgiven and forgotten. I am free in this moment."

*It's not the cards
you're dealt,
of course.
It's
how you play
them.*

NAL

Tarot

I read tarot when I was in my twenties, the Rider-Waite deck, and then I stopped. I've since picked it up again. I took a class from Carol Barbeau on the Osho Zen deck. This deck has a very kind, gentle energy. There are still the four suits: rainbow, water/emotions, fire, and clouds. There is a Major Arcana. There are seventy-nine cards in the Osho Zen deck and these are each very intuitive. Clouds can represent what others have told you, ideas taught to you that cloud your own perception of what truly is. Water/emotion cards are self-explanatory and include cards such as "healing" and "letting go." In the rainbow suit there's a card for Abundance that pictures a man sitting on what may be the Book of Knowledge and wearing a dressing gown open at the chest along with a big smile. Then, there's Ordinariness, featuring a girl carrying a basket full of flowers and walking through a spring meadow with trees abloom and all seems ever so tranquil. Then, there is the card called Maturity where the silhouette of a woman is depicted, filled not with skin and bones but with flowers and above her head is dead wood as though the flowers have matured and died. A beautiful daisy represents her forehead and there is a rainbow circle surrounding her head, the outside of which is a serpent that I think represents knowledge and healing.

    Sometimes, I'll shuffle the cards until a card falls out and then I'll meditate on that card for a while. Other times, I'll do an entire Celtic Cross, or I'll do a three card spread where the first card, the middle card, represents the now, the second card, placed before the middle card, is the foundation of the question, and the last card, placed after the middle card, represents the future. Then, you can lay remaining cards to represent thirty-day increments. This can be very enlightening. There's also an astrological layout where the cards are laid out according to the twelve houses of the zodiac.

    Since returning to tarot, I wanted to learn more about the protocols of the art. I started with The Complete Idiot's

Guide to Tarot, second edition, by Arlene Tognetti and Lisa Lenard. I was turned on to this by my friend Trish Holmes who loaned me one of Arlene's books, Intuitive Arts On Money (co-written by Katherine A. Gleason.) I found this book so intriguing and Arlene's style so inviting that I decided to start learning to read Tarot from the beginning. I'm enjoying learning more and more about tarot and how it speaks to me. There is so much to be learned, and it seems like one of the most important things to learn is to let the ego step aside so that spirit can come through. For me, that is the most difficult part, I think.

It's easy for me to consider what's coming through, to judge it and to think of it with a logical bent and of course one cannot do that with tarot. Sometimes I fall into a kind of comparison trap. That other person owns their own home and I've lost mine. That other person has more formal education than I do and so that makes them a more enlightened individual. The list of bullshit goes on and on, when allowed to continue. I just have to thank my mind and ego for their interest and tell them I'm concentrating on something else now, and then concentrate only on allowing helpful energy to come through.

I've also been experimenting with different tarot card decks. What fun! A recent trip to Stargazers in Bellevue brought me to a lovely exchange with a friend of mine from an astrology group that I've found. I'd gone that evening to listen to a lecture by the Portland-based astrologer Mark Dodich, and I found a beautiful tarot deck using images from Botticelli's paintings. Its energy is very hot and active. My friend found a deck she liked, the Motherpeace Deck, and so, having been told at some point that tarot speaks more easily to you when the deck has been a gift, we purchased each other's deck and had a little gifting ceremony in the store. It made for a very nice memory and the beginning of what seems to be a wonderful energy in these cards.

*Once upon a time,
in a land far away,
there was a woman
who was lost
on her road.*

NAL

Mythic Journaling

I'd seen the advertisement in the Sunday paper for a class being held at Crystal Voyage, a local bookstore, and immediately called to register. When I walked in, there were several long portable tables set up with different fairy tale books and a supply of index cards, pens, and pencils. The class was an hour and a half. The first half hour was spent with introductions. The presenter was Becka Mordini, a life coach.

Becka looked like she could be a professional dancer. She had long straight black hair and was dressed that evening all in black. For the life of me, I don't remember exactly what she wore, only that her demeanor seemed very warm, and grounded, and full of strength.

First taught under the name of Fairy Tale Magic, Becka later changed the name to Mythic Journaling as she developed this as one of several programs she has created that "help people to shift their perspectives to create greater power in their lives," as Ms. Mordini puts it. Ms. Mordini explained that she tries to help people to see alternate choices in their lives, to open new avenues of awareness.

During the next three fifteen-minute sessions, we started our own fairy tale. First, we wrote a short story in which we were a character in a fairy tale of our choice. In the second session we rewrote the same story, but this time we had power objects that we could use, such as shields that made us invisible, or a powder that enabled us to fly, or animals with special powers. During the last rewrite, the instruction was to write the story and make ourselves the hero, the winner.

I chose Rapunzel and here is my story.

Once upon a time there lived a lovely princess with long, grey hair. She lived in a tall castle made of polished river rock high above the hills and far away from other castles. She had a wicked stepfather who yelled at her when she left her toys out while she was creating and who laughed at her creations because they were just not good enough in his eyes. His name was King John.

King John carried three big keys on his belt and with one he locked Rapunzel away. She was only allowed out of her prison when he was in the mood to cook. Then, he would let her come out to eat the food he'd prepared. Except for that, she remained locked in the castle. Rapunzel called from her window every day, but no one came. One day, an angel on a tall white horse rode away from the nearby road and through the meadow near Rapunzel's castle and, hearing Rapunzel's cry, spread her magical wings and took her to a beautiful village where she could nurture her inner children, her creativity.

I hadn't realized this before, this sense of being locked away. I did lock myself away from so many things I loved. The result was a slow death of all my talents from the effects of verbal abuse, and my choice in how I handled that abuse. Of course, these qualities inside me didn't die; they just lay dormant, like fields allowed to fallow.

Here is how I spent the second fifteen minutes. Same setting, but this time...

Rapunzel was commanded by the King to share a meal and for dessert he chose a juicy apple, a piece of fruit like any other in the bowl ... but this one made him fall asleep. Rapunzel, seeing her opportunity, took his big sword from the wall and laid it by her chain. Then, stealthily, she reached for the keys on the King's belt. He had eaten a big meal and had taken off his belt to be more comfortable. Armed with the sword lest he wake, Rapunzel unlocked the castle door and left the castle and grounds forever.

She was lucky to meet a group of dwarves on her way who helped her to find a new castle and they all became very good friends. When the dwarves walked to the new castle with Rapunzel, they told her stories of the villagers she would meet. She became so excited that it was hard to know whom to meet and get to know first. There was Lulu, the writer, and Capulet the actor, and there was the lady with the big hat who bought and sold property and had agreed to help Rapunzel find just the right castle.

In her new castle, Rapunzel found a box covered with gold and jewels. Another new friend, Hecate, came to introduce herself. Hecate had owned the box before and she had the key. Together, they opened the box and Hecate showed Rapunzel the snow globes inside. Hecate drew them out, one by one, each snow globe showing a different little scene for Rapunzel to explore. Rapunzel writing, acting, painting, working, helping others. Rapunzel lived to be very old and she never did decide what she wanted to be. She did all of those things that she wanted to do and she liked who she'd become.

*Magnificence
is already within you.
Just
acknowledge it.*

NAL

Astrology

I was turned on to astrology shortly after my divorce, when I was really feeling at loose ends with my life, and researching for direction. About this time, my daughter asked me if I'd ever had my astrological chart done. No, I hadn't. She recommended Ro Laughan, an astrologer in California, so I contacted her. Her fee was $150 and she needed a two-hour telephone call with me. She would be out of town for the next two weeks and she had May 12th at 11:00 available. I did some research on the internet to find out if her price was in line and found that many other sites were charging $250 and up.

First, Ro needed the exact date and time of my birth. There is no hour expressed on the copy of the birth certificate that I had, so I reached out to family members for information. My older sister remembered that my father had called at a quarter past twelve on the twelfth of October to tell the family that I had been born. Ro's basic premise was that I am here to shine my light. What does that mean? I have so many things I want to do. What is shining my light? On what? Where? On whom? Did I want to go back to school and finish my degree? What is it that I want to do with my life? Where do I want to be in five years? In ten years? In twenty years? What is it that I like? What do I like to read? What do I like to listen to? I was about to do some exploring.

My conversation with Ro set off an interest in astrology that led me to pursue it in other ways. I found a CD that sounded interesting called The Moon and You: Using the Lunar Phases to Create a Magical Life by the astrologer Carol Barbeau. This was great information, about knowing what to anticipate in yourself and other people and how to use the cycles of the moon to your best advantage. Grow things at the new moon, release things at the full moon. What did I want to grow and nurture? Was it love, especially love of myself, and kindness, especially kindness to myself? What did I want to release? I wanted to release self-doubt and procrastination. This CD led me to another by Ms. Barbeau, Moon: Doorway to Past Lives and Future Possibilities. This led me to yet another, and another, and then I was taking classes with her and learning more and more about astrology, about my motivations and the cycles of my life, what to anticipate and how to best work with energies in the sky as the planets transit through the various houses of my natal chart.

During my first astrological reading with Carol Barbeau, she could tell by comparing my natal chart with that of my ex-husband that we have been together in several lifetimes and we've killed each other before. Sometimes, I have been the woman, and sometimes I have been the man. Sometimes, I have been the killer; others, I have been the one killed. Grisly, isn't it? Imagine if I would have had my chart done before I married this man! I don't know, though, I was pretty in love with him. I don't know if I would have stood still long enough for anything to sink in. I was so captivated by him. Maybe this was one reason I could always see the wounded child in him, as well as other things.

What I've learned from astrology is helpful to me every day. I keep an ephemeris at hand. This tells me the position of the planets on a daily basis. Combined with the mental image of my own natal chart, it is easier for me to understand my feelings, actions and reactions.

I enjoy it when the moon, the planet of emotion, is in Aries every month because I can count on having more energy to take action. I find it easier to have fun and be creative when the moon makes its monthly transit into Leo. I tend to be more artsy when the moon shifts into Libra. And, if I'm going to make a presentation or something on a day the moon is in Capricorn, I make extra sure that I'm well prepared and know my audience. Yes, I do plan some of my activities around what the planets are doing because I feel I will be more successful.

I get an astrological reading at least once a year, for my year ahead. And, did you know that you can also choose what kind of year you're going to have? To some degree, anyway, you can choose what kind of a year you will have by changing your location for the period twenty-four hours before the time of your birth and then you can leave just after the hour of your birth. It's a little like being reborn, or voting. You set yourself up as a "resident" of that longitude and latitude during that twenty-four hour period before your solar return. Then, at the time of your birth, you're setting up your year as though you were born in that latitude and longitude, on that time and date, because of how the planets land in the various houses of your astrological chart. This takes a professional astrologer and it's called astro-cartography. At the suggestion of Carol Barbeau, I've celebrated my birthday in Honolulu and Philadelphia, and this year I get to celebrate it right here in Seattle/Tacoma because that's what shows up as best for me in my chart. Note: the date and time of your solar return varies from your actual birthday. Because of the earth's rotation, the sun may return to the exact position it was at your birth on a day or two before or after your actual calendar birthday.

I have a big event coming up in my life a year from next month. On September 26, 2011, the planet Saturn will return to the exact degree that it was at the time of my birth. This is called a Saturn Return and it happens roughly every twenty-nine and a half years. Saturn, as well as other planets, is also important for things during transit. Saturn is a taskmaster. It makes you work, but if you do the work, it helps you receive the recognition and rewards. Carol Barbeau has suggested that I go to Denver for this event because it changes the houses in which the planets appear. In other words, it changes the manner in which those planetary energies express themselves in my life. Because this is said to set up, basically, the next twenty-nine years of my life, I'm paying attention.

There are mixed opinions among astrologers about astro-cartography, and one reason is because planetary influences carry an arc of influence. For example, Saturn carries a long arc of influence. The influence of this Saturn return I've mentioned actually began a year or so before the event. Going to Washington, D.C., Philadelphia, and Honolulu for my solar return changed the houses where the planets would express themselves during the coming year. For instance, in the astrological sixth house, planets express themselves as work, duty, service and health, or the need or wish for attention to matters of health. I would rather have those influences express themselves in the seventh house of various kinds of partnerships—in other words, people wanting to help me instead of expecting me to help them. So, yes, I'm doing this again, this year, by going to Denver for my Saturn return, because the process, as I've used it in the past for my solar return, seemed effective. I am willing to make a leap of faith and pay a visit to Denver.

I was such a skeptic at first, and even when I lost my skepticism, I still had very little faith and trust until I began to have faith and trust in myself again. When I first started exploring astrology and the transits, what life would be bringing to me, I thought that everything I was learning about the future would be bad and I didn't want to see bad things. Slowly, I've come to realize that it's my spin on life, how I choose to see the world. I can choose to see the good, and only the good, or to see the bad and know beyond doubt that good will come from it. It always does. My life is up to me. Even the incident with my spouse, I was part of that. Because I chose not to own my own power, I attracted a violent situation. I am responsible. I am not a victim. I am responsible to myself for showing up in my own life and conducting my life in such a way as to decrease the likelihood that this type of situation will occur again. We never really know when something bad like an abuse is going to happen to us, but there are signs we can see if we maintain strength to look. And, because I know I am responsible, I can choose to handle my life with joy and with commitment to myself and my own values. I am so thankful to these tools and the people I've come to know during this exploration.

This reminds me of something I saw recently on a video put out by Louise Hay. She was offering an alternative suggestion to how people might handle a problem, or a situation they perceived may be a problem. Her suggestion was to repeat this affirmation, "All is well. Everything is working out for my highest good. Out of this situation, only good will come. And I am safe." I like this. I'll try this. Thank you, Ms. Hay.

*Talk to me.
I'm here.
You're here.
Life is waiting.
But not for long.
Tarry not.*

NAL

My Favorite Tarot Reader

Lou J. Free is one of my favorite tarot readers. She works with a deck of plain playing cards, and what she told me was, "You're being blocked. You may have feng shui'd your apartment, but you need to physically go through your house and check out everything that could possibly have your ex-husband's energy on it. Either throw it away or give it away; or, if you want to keep it, then imagine it engulfed in white light, a circle of white light and bless it by saying, 'This has only my energy now.' That includes photographs and furniture, anything." I burst out laughing, then, because it occurred to me that I still hadn't updated a tattoo that I have on my chest. My ex-husband has a tattoo with my name on it, and I have a tattoo that has his name on it. They're both the same thing: a short stemmed red rose with the name on a banner that crosses the stem. The very next morning saw me searching the net for tattoo parlors in Tacoma. My search led me to House of Tattoo on Sixth Avenue one week later where, after only half an hour, I left with a new armored plating above my left breast. The $70 I paid was more than worth it in exchange for a renewed feeling of empowerment.

      The other comment that Lou made to me was that, when I'm thinking of my ex-husband, he's likely thinking of me as well. She suggested I think of a ricochet and just send those thoughts back to him, not owning any of them. My life is my life now, and it doesn't belong to anyone else. I value the boundaries that I've created with friends and loved ones, I value my ability to set boundaries and express myself authentically. I continue to learn and grow, and that's icing on the cake, because I am already complete and valuable, just as I am at this second and I require no outside validation

*Hey!
Stop cooking!
You're done!*

NAL

Body Work, Again: Colon Hydrotherapy

Wooh! I'm just beginning to learn about colonics. When I was growing up, I was taught about enemas. Ooh, this is really ghastly stuff to share, or at least it is for me. But, the thought of the variety of diseases that can come directly from autointoxication, or self-poisoning, makes me want to share it here. Unlike the other things I've shared in this book, I will not be sharing my experiences about this. I will say that the procedure is not unpleasant, one's modesty is maintained, and the benefits far outweigh any inconvenience.

The main function of the colon, a tube about five feet long and two and a half inches in diameter, is to eliminate digestive residue and rid the body of toxins and waste. Another word for the large intestine, the colon has several parts including the transverse, ascending and descending colons. To paraphrase from a pamphlet provided by my colon hydrotherapy worker, Dee Rowe, consuming mucous-producing foods such as red meat, dairy products, and flour can cause dense, sticky bowel movements. "These stools leave behind a glue-like coating on the wall of the colon which accumulates layer-by-layer into a hard, rubbery crust. The body cannot eliminate this on its own—colon hydrotherapy can help remove this from the body."

I've been told by my physician that colon cancer is the most easily prevented cancer. My stools (if you share this with anyone else, I am going to find you) seemed pretty dense, my skin didn't seem as lively as it once did, and it seemed like I just couldn't get enough fiber or exercise to change it. I'd learned about Dee Rowe from my sister first, then from my friend Trish. I finally gave her a call and went in for a treatment. Dee is also a licensed massage therapist and she certainly knows her stuff when it comes to nutrition and the care of the colon. Directly from Dee's brochure: "The colon is the largest perpetrator of disease of any organ in the body and is said to be the initiator of 80% of all critical illnesses."

As for my experience, I've had to go back once, so two treatments, and since then I've been much more mindful of the amount of fiber I'm taking in every day. I've always tried to drink plenty of water. I'm told the best amount is half your body weight in ounces. In fact, I bought one of those steel bottles years ago just so I could keep track of my water intake. It holds forty ounces of water and I drink at least one a day, more when I'm lifting weights.

I asked Dee, "What is the best food to maintain a healthy colon?" She replied, "The colon loves beets." She suggested raw beets or baked, but not canned. I've never been a beet lover. In fact, during the summer when I buy my vegetables at the Proctor Farmers' Market, I have always tried to find someone who likes beets and hates beet greens so we can swap. Because of Dee's suggestion, though, I tried grated raw beets on a salad and I fell in love. The sweetness contrasts with the tanginess of the dressing (I used blue cheese dressing). I'm a convert.

Kale is good for your large intestine and apple is good for your small intestine. You can't go wrong with an apple a day, and apple and lemon are two fruits you can combine with any other food. Other fruit, Dee reminded me, should be eaten on an empty stomach and not combined with protein, grain, or dairy because of the time it takes for protein, grain, and dairy to be digested. If fruit has to stop and digest with other foods it becomes fermented in the process and you not only lose the antioxidant properties, but you increase the likelihood of gas and bloating.

Trust me.
It's a great world out there.
Just get out in it and make it yours.
Listen. Be a part of it.
If it turns out to be not so great,
find a different world,
get out in it, and make it yours.
Repeat as necessary.

NAL

EFT

A group of like-minded friends grew out of our participation in several of Carol Barbeau's astrology classes. We gather once a month to share our talents, and often just our friendship. It was my privilege last month to learn of a technique from our presenter, Nancy Muth, that I'd not been exposed to, or even heard of, before.

EFT, which stands for Emotional Freedom Techniques, is a combination of tapping a series of acupressure points on your face and body, intent, and words to break the emotional loop of brain/body sensations. According to their website, this technique can be used for weight loss; ridding oneself of addiction; emotional issues; pain, disease and physical issues, and "everything else."

Nancy's presentation was very simple, showing us just the basic recipe for using this technique. I encourage you to go to the EFT website to learn more about this, rather than go into it here. That website is: www.EFTUniverse.com.

Here is a transcript of a recording I did following one of my first EFT sessions as a client. I recorded this with Dragon technology and I think it's worth sharing. It's tough to explain how EFT works.

> I feel like I've had a paradigm shift, a renaissance of some sort. My body is tingling all over. It's just tingling. I've just left the home of my EFT practitioner following an EFT session and we worked on…. What did we work on? I mean, it was everything from…. It started over the fact that I was hesitant to practice languages, practice my Spanish, practice my French, practice my tarot reading, because I wanted to be proficient—first—and of course you can't become proficient without practicing. So then she asked, "Where did that come from?" She meant this feeling of being perfect from the start. I realized it was from a lot

of things when I was growing up. You know, my mother saying things like "It's better to have some people think you're stupid instead of to open your mouth and prove it." I suppose, and hope, that parents are more enlightened now, but when I was growing up I heard a lot of clichés. And then there were some other childhood memories. We tapped on those beliefs, those memories, and those feelings that I took and internalized from those memories. I had a huge shift, then, and a huge acceptance of myself, and a huge appreciation for my process.

After the final tapping, I had an image in my mind of breaking glass, of a thick glass window. The glass was like two or three feet thick and all of a sudden it just broke, by itself. It broke into big shards of glass, and then I was reminded of losing my virginity and remembered when my hymen broke. The feeling I ultimately got out of this EFT session was that I was safe. I am safe. I am a grown up. I can trust myself. I can set healthy boundaries. I can trust that process that is life. I can trust. I mean, so I get a Spanish word wrong. Too bad, at least I'm trying. I'm being out there. I'm living my life, I'm not medicating it. I'm not throwing a cover over it. I'm allowing myself to feel and I can allow myself to feel because I am secure in who I am and I can take care of myself. I can take care of my own emotional needs, my own physical needs. I can be open to that.

I can see as a direct resultof my work with EFT that I'm opening up more and more, and I'm becoming more and more creative. I'm having more trust in myself. I'm risking more. I'm open. I'm just so much more open to myself and appreciative of myself.

It's interesting to see where so many of our beliefs come from. Sometimes they come from a place where we formed a belief or a pattern of thought, say, as a three-year-old, a five-year-old, or a ten-year-old. From that one little kernel, from that one little belief we've attached short threads or long threads, maybe many threads from other experiences as we've grown older that tie in with that same thing. We just keep reinforcing it, over and over, as we react to triggers. In EFT this is referred to as "writing on the walls," where you have a belief and then you attract similar incidents to support the original belief, even if that belief no longer serves you.

EFT slices through that energy like an arrow. Today it was like a big cannonball—just, boom, right through that thick glass wall—and then I had this almost orgasmic feeling, a sensation of release all over my body. I nearly passed out. I was getting dizzy because of the movement of energy in my body. It was magnificent.

I've become so enamored of this technique that I'm now pursuing certification as a practitioner. This is such a wonderful, and powerful, tool. Since it enables me to challenge my old beliefs, to address my motivations in a more honest fashion, and to update my beliefs to more closely support my current goals and lifestyle, it's perfect for including in this book about reinventing me.

Here are some of the things that were written on my wall. Gary Craig, founder of EFT, calls our brain the "palace of possibilities" wherein there are thousands of rooms. Because of our limiting beliefs—experiences we interpreted according to the age and circumstance when we had those experiences—we often spend our lives in just one room. I'm tapping on these writings on my wall, and wondering if perhaps you may have experienced similar writing on your own walls.

You're a lazy good for nothing, said Mom.

You don't know how to take care of anything, said Mom.

You don't take care of anything, said Mom when she came into my room one day and saw a mess on the floor.

I'll give you something to cry about.

When I was seven years old, I was left at the airport with no one to pick me up. I felt abandoned, unwanted, and unloved. I felt so scared that something had happened to my mom. I felt like I was supposed to take care of myself, but I didn't know how. I felt like I was supposed to be a grown up, but I didn't know how. I looked happy and calm and confident on the outside but on the inside I was scared to death. When I first tapped on this, the intensity was an eight based on the EFT scale of zero through then. The second round of tapping brought the intensity down to a two. I hadn't realized how much this memory meant to me.

You don't listen. My mom said this to me hundreds of times.

She's too small, get her out of here, said Dad.

      Sometimes it's easier to hold on to our old beliefs, because when we give them up, what are we without them? We have to choose what to replace them with. I chose empowerment recently, after a discussion with a woman named Mary who I met in Chicago. She was a—yes, I admit it, I sought out still another clairvoyant—she told me she had power and she was willing to share it with me. If, that is, I let her tell me what to write, what to publish, when to publish, etc. Turns out, I wasn't interested in what she had to offer. I didn't want her power in my life. I wanted my power in my life. I didn't want my life to be "solved." I wanted my life to be lived. She told me not to be so open, not to share everything in my life. I want to share. I want people to know about how some of these modalities feel when you're going through them. I want to share. I don't want to be separate and apart from people. I don't want others to be separate and apart from me. We are all one. Separateness is only an illusion that we maintain to protect ourselves, which it doesn't.

*Thank you, God,
for this opportunity to express
your love and creativity flowing
through me. Giving, taking,
exploring space, I dance in this
world, in step with you—and
you—and you....*

NAL

Dance

I used to like to dance. And, I was told I was a good dancer. As I recall, it wasn't always a family member who made that statement. My mother hated ironing, so when I was in high school, I would trade with my mother: I'd do the ironing to earn a late night during the week so I could go to a dance. I did this a lot. Now, this wasn't ballroom dancing, but it was still following a partner and an occasional jitterbug or lindy hop. My parents divorced when I was six or seven years old, and after that I visited my father every year. He was a master baker who had apprenticed and mastered his trade in Sweden, and then moved to Alaska for the good money it paid. He worked for several years as the head baker at the hotel in Nome. After that, he moved to Valdez, and then to Juneau. My mother taught me a lot of dance steps. Every Saturday evening while I lived at home, we would turn on my mother's favorite program, the Lawrence Welk Show, and we would very often dance together around our small living room. Alaska was where I really practiced dancing, though.

One of my favorite memories is when I was staying with my sister Sonja in Anchorage. She owned an old roadhouse about fifty miles outside of Anchorage called Teikel. We stayed there for a couple of weeks one summer, and we ventured to Valdez over a weekend to see my Dad. I guess I was about twelve or fourteen. One night, we went to this tavern in the neighborhood. Don't think of a neighborhood like you see when you look out your living room window. It was more like a village, in the tundra. Anyway, there were a lot of guys there. I think they worked in the oil fields. I didn't know or really care what they did. I drank a dozen or so Roy Rogers—you know, one of the two preferred drinks of children, then at least, (a Shirley Temple being the other one)—and we danced. We danced 'til 4:00 in the morning. It was such a good time.

When I was about nineteen, and I lived and worked in Juneau. I lived with a girlfriend first, in a one-bedroom apartment on Auk Bay. Then, when she moved out to live with a local firefighter she'd fallen in love with, I had the place to myself for a month and then moved in with my dad. We used to go dancing at the Baranof Hotel. My dad was five foot five and probably weighed a hundred pounds, or maybe a hundred and ten. Although he was twenty-one when he emigrated from Sweden, he still had a heavy accent. I think he liked that the accent gave him added panache. I was always disappointed he didn't teach us kids how to speak Swedish, and I was very fortunate to have learned it, but much later.

On at least one occasion I remember, Dad and I went dancing. Dad was a regular at the Baranof and I think he tipped well. Plus, he was just generally a nice and gregarious man, full of passion for life and for living. The band played a Swedish waltz; Dad and I moved out onto the floor. No one joined us. Dad used the floor like he'd bought it the week before. Gads, I remember him looking at me, as if to say, "Just keep it up honey. Pay attention and don't screw it up." I was so nervous because I knew what a proud man he was. He just wanted to complete a professional presentation. And, fortunately, we did. The other guests and diners applauded as we left the floor. It was quite the experience. Years later, I was devastated when I realized that my dad had either baker's disease or emphysema and was no longer able to dance with me. I was in my early twenties, and suddenly I felt all alone because I could feel my father leaving me behind and going on a different journey.

But, on that night, he danced beautifully, with a command of the floor and a command of his partner incongruent with his stature. We walked back to his apartment after we'd closed up the Baranof. It was a cool evening in late fall, and we stopped on the way to get a warm donut at the bakery where Dad worked as a pastry chef. The donut, a crueler that we ate warm during the walk home, is a taste I shall always remember.

Still one more dance memory I have occurred when I was four or five years old. I actually wrote a poem about it when

I was twenty-five and into writing poems. My parents loved to dance. My mother always said that if they could just have stayed on the dance floor, she and my father would have never divorced. But, my dad was a baker. And, my mother was his partner in business as well as in life, and in life it didn't work out so very well. But, on this one Christmas that I remember very well, I watched them dance and it was beautiful.

Every Christmas, as I recall, my family would gather at our house. There was my grandfather Alfred, my mother's dad, and his wife Pearl, the only grandmother I ever knew. Pearl was wonderful. She was warm, and loving, and kind. She used to like to drink a beer and watch the fights. She married my grandfather, who I understood from my mother and aunt to have been a man who could sing all night without repeating a song. When I knew him, he had had an operation on his throat and, during the surgery, the surgeon's knife had slipped, cutting his vocal chords, and he lost his ability to speak. This must have been a hell on earth for him. And it was this man whom this warm and loving woman married and whose family she accepted as her own—me, at least. I don't know about the others because I was too young.

At Christmas, in addition to my grandparents, there were my sisters, Rosalie, Sonja and Gloria, and my brother Ronald. Then, my mother's sister, Aunt Rosalie, and her husband Tom, and I think that was it. It was our custom to each provide some kind of entertainment. My Aunt Rosalie told a story. My sisters sang a song. Then, it was time for my parents to provide some diversion. We lived in a big white house in Potlatch, Washington. There was the living room, two bedrooms, bathroom, and kitchen on the ground floor, and then another two bedrooms upstairs. The living room was long, almost the whole length of the house. I think my parents were attracted to it because it looked like a good dance floor.

Well, on that delectable Christmas night, my uncle moved the furniture up against the wall and my parents danced. They did the Schottische, and the Ham bow, and the Swedish waltz. I looked up at them and they were beauty in motion. They were our own Fred Astaire and Ginger Rogers. They used to call my father Legs Larson. He was a great leader and my mother was a great follower.

So, now, as I move back into social circles, I am once again at that awful awkward stage. That stage when you're just learning something new. I felt like a self-conscious and clumsy teenager.

To get through this, I signed up for a series of private dance lessons with Natasha Thayer. Natasha is an internationally known title holder who owns and operates Studio 6 Ballroom in Tacoma. She is fun and warm, nurturing and supportive—and, of course, a wonderful dancer. Scared and excited, I arrived at her studio and slowly but surely I am learning the nuances of partner dancing. She teaches from technique up to styling, and beyond. I have a very sound foundation, and I try to practice technique every day. One of my new goals is to dance in competition. Oh, wouldn't that be fun? Wow. A lot of work, but I think it would be a lot of fun too. Too bad there's no money in dancing.

This is a fun activity you too might like to try. There's USA Dance Club all across the country, and then there's the Elks, and the Eagles, and various Swing Clubs. There's probably a singles dance club in your town or surrounding area. It can be a great workout, and a great way to meet and get to know people. Here in the greater Seattle area, there's a dance somewhere every night of the week. You get to know people. They become part of your community. See the information in the references section of this book for additional information about how you can get connected with some people who like to have fun.

Epilogue

When I think of the tools and people to whom I've been exposed during the last several years, including those I was resistant to at first, I'm reminded of that story about the man who dies in a flood. A dam has broken and the waters are rushing through this small town. The man goes to the lanai of his house and asks God for help. A young man and small girl row by and ask the man if he wants a ride to safety. "No," says the man, "I'm okay, children, God will save me." The waters continue to rise and the man climbs to his rooftop. He sees a dog clinging to a log as it moves rapidly along and he cries, "God, save me." Along comes a policeman who says, "Everybody out of their homes, sir, we have to evacuate the area." The man, so sure of his faith in a loving God, replies, "I understand that, son, and I'll be gone in just a moment." Next, we see him standing at the pearly gates of heaven and he asks St. Peter, "Why didn't God save me?" St. Peter replies, "What do you mean, why didn't God save you? Didn't He send George and Susie in their rowboat?" "Oh," the man responded, "that was God who sent them?" St. Peter went on, "Didn't He send Officer Howard?" "Oh," the man said again, "that was God who sent him?" As for me, I don't always listen, whether it's God or my spirit guides or fairy godmother or whomever that speaks so lovingly to me and leads me, but I do know that knowledge and direction come to us in a lot of different packages.

    The main thing I've been doing with all of these tools is honoring myself, all of myself. For years I thought that being unfinished was a bad thing. I don't know why, but that was my perception. I remember a painting I got from a friend who was moving out of state. It was an oil painting that appeared to me to have just been begun. It's been many years ago now, but I remember that it was framed. Maybe it was, in fact, a finished piece. I only recall that, for some thirty years I thought of myself as unfinished. I identified with that painting. Now, I understand this is what I'm all about. I'm always learning, I'm always trying new things. We're not intended to be finished. We are complete already, and valuable. I am wonderful just as I am, today. And so, dearest reader, are you. The news that you are complete and valuable may come to you any number of ways. For me, it's Louise Hay telling us to look in the mirror and honestly affirm, several times a day, "I love you" and Carol Barbeau, showing me how to anticipate and make better use of the energies of the stars. All of these continue to help me become a better person, a more fulfilled and joyful person.

      Oh gads! Sometimes I catch myself still doing this not honoring myself thing. I'm working at the state fair, right. I mean, I've taken this minimum wage … oh, sorry, it's not minimum wage, it is $.35 above minimum wage, at the fair. I leave work and on the way out, I am so hungry I could eat my arm when I think to myself, "Oh, how about one of those barbeque sandwiches, I could stop and have one of those." They're $7. I decide that I can wait until I get home. Next, I'm called to a juicy hamburger with fried onions. The sensation of onions melting their gorgeous sweetness in my mouth as I walk is palpable; I'm salivating. I decide I can wait until I get home. I walk to the employee parking lot and get into my car and I think to myself, "Self, in the overall scheme of things, how important was that hamburger, or that sandwich? It was a moment that I allowed myself to miss out on when I really could have stopped to eat something and considered that as a kind of ritual, openly honoring myself and expressing love for myself for under $10, and I chose not to." I'm thinking rather Zen here, you know, it's not good and it's not bad. It just is. Yet, as I ponder all of the ways that I tried to honor myself when I first left my old environment, I want to make sure to continue and even deepen that trend. I'm listening to old astrology tapes now, to the readings that I had during and just after my divorce, and I feel like a butterfly.

Learning...and, living!

Is there life after recovery? Can I imagine being touched by another man? That's an awfully long time to be with someone, those years I spent with my ex-husband.

    I'm still looking for the right man, but I'm starting to have fun with the process. I don't need another man to feel complete, or to survive. But, it would be pleasant to share experiences with a like-minded human being. Yes, I was nervous at first. I don't know if it was the era I was raised in or what. I finally faced the fact that I used sex for a variety of reasons, and not always for what was good for me. I used it as an escape. I used it as a way of surviving. I could use it to even say thank you. Hmm . . . that's changed. I still consider sex to be a really good thing, but it is certainly not the be-all and end-all in a relationship. Whether it's do it yourself strategies or abstinence, once I started honoring myself in other ways, sex went to its appropriate place in my life.

    I have to share that my first post-divorce relationship, even though I had waited six years, still mirrored a rebound relationship. I moved too fast. I didn't listen as well as I should have, to him, or to myself. I wasn't able to remain friends with this person, and I regret this because he's a nice man. But, I learned a lot about myself in the process. One of the things I learned was I'm still okay. I'm wonderful. I can set boundaries and I can take care of myself, and as I have more relationships, I'm going to do this better and better.

    Now, I have several men with whom I'm friends, just friends. I like men again, they're nice people. I can appreciate them because I can appreciate me.

    I don't know where I would be if it wasn't for these tools. It's taken me quite a while to explore them and of course I'm not finished. I realize that I'm planning my tomorrows, and with the arrival of a few tomorrows I'll be, again, a changed person. And, that changed person will be a springboard to yet another changed person. I embrace this process called life! It is indeed the process and not the destination that matters because, after all, it is the destination that is always changing. We may not realize it at first, but it does, beautifully. Given time, you will come to know that too. Here's a toast to the beauty that is you!

Namaste

Helpful Resources

National Domestic Violence Hotline
1-800-799-SAFE; TTY 1-800-787-3224
info@YWCA.org

Trish Holmes with Sound Financial Concepts
Credit related information generously shared by permission from Trish Holmes of Sound Financial Concepts, "a Doug Holmes Company."
http://seemoney.com/ Local: trishh@wamail.net
Local: 253 272-1114 or Toll Free: 800 473-5495
P. O. Box 8880 Tacoma, WA 98419-0880

Carol Barbeau with Illuminations Astrology
www. Carolbarbeau.com
carolastro@carolbarbeau.com

Lou J. Free, Ph.D.c.CHT
www.ParadiseWest.com
TexasWind9@aol.com

Dale Golden, MSW, ACSW, LICSW, CHTP
Local: 253 752-2516
goldendale@aol.com

Dorothy Lynn, Intuitive Counselor
angelsallaround@vzw.blackberry.net
253 272-7337 or 253 732-7337 (SEER)

Becka Mordini with Mythic Journaling
www.mythicjournaling.com

info@YWCA.org

USA Dance
Call 800-447-9047
or visit them online at usadance.org for your own local information

Seattle Swing Club
visit them at seattlewcswing.org

Eagles
Go to www.foe.com
to locate the chapters nearest you.

Elks
You can call their main office in Chicago at 773 755-4700 or visit their website, www.elks.org, and click on the State Association tab for information for your local area.

Books Referenced

Goddesses in Older Women:
Archetypes in Women over Fifty
by Jean Shinoda Bolen

Visual Journaling:
Going Deeper than Words
by Barbara Ganim & Susan Fox
1999 Quest Books
ISBN: 0-8356-0777-1

You Can Heal Your Life
by Louise Hay
ISBN: 1-56160-628-0

The Feng Shui of Abundance:
A Practical and Spiritual Guide to Attracting Wealth into Your
Life
By Suzan Hilton
ISBN: 978-0767907507

SoulCollage® Evolving
An Intuitive Collage Process for Self-Discovery & Community
by Seena B. Frost
ISBN: 0-9643158-4-X

The Complete Idiot's Guide to Tarot, second edition
Arlene Tognetti and Lisa Lenard
ISBN: 978-1-59257-066-9

Anatomy of the Spirit:
the Seven Stages of Power and Healing
Caroline Myss, PH.D.
ISBN: 0-609-80014-0

Autobiography of a Yogi
by Paramahansa Yogananda

Audio Books and CDs Referenced

The Moon and You: Using Lunar Phases to Create a Magical Life
by Carol Barbeau

The Moon: Doorway to Past Lives and Future Possibilities
by Carol Barbeau

Tarot Decks Referenced

Golden Botticelli Tarot
By Lo Scarabeo with Botticelli illustrations

Motherpeace Round Tarot Deck
by Karen Vogel and Vicki Noble

Rider Tarot Deck
by Arthur Edward Waite, illustrated by Pamela Coleman Smith

Osho Zen Tarot
Osho. Original illustrations by Ma Deva Padma
1994 St Martin's Press

.

www.ingramcontent.com/pod-product-compliance
Lightning Source LLC
Chambersburg PA
CBHW061951070426
42450CB00007BA/1188